1 MONTH OF
FREE
READING

at
www.ForgottenBooks.com

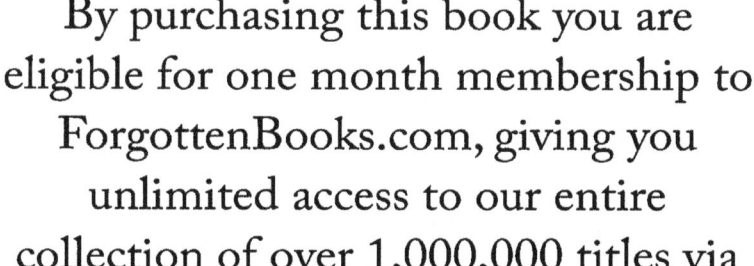

By purchasing this book you are eligible for one month membership to ForgottenBooks.com, giving you unlimited access to our entire collection of over 1,000,000 titles via our web site and mobile apps.

To claim your free month visit:

www.forgottenbooks.com/free435648

ISBN 978-0-365-06004-8
PIBN 10435648

Forgotten Books is a registered trademark of FB &c Ltd.
Copyright © 2018 FB &c Ltd.
FB &c Ltd, Dalton House, 60 Windsor Avenue, London, SW19 2RR.
Company number 08720141. Registered in England and Wales.

For support please visit www.forgottenbooks.com

The
Early Massachusetts Press
1638–1711

The Early

Massachusetts Press

1638–1711

By

George Emery Littlefield

In Two Volumes

Vol. II

Boston, Massachusetts

The Club of Odd Volumes

1907

Contents

Illustrations

The Early Massachusetts Press
1638–1711

John Foster

The
Early Massachusetts Press
1638–1711

𝕵𝖔𝖍𝖓 𝕱𝖔𝖘𝖙𝖊𝖗

THE press which Marmaduke Johnson had been permitted to set up in Boston, nine years after his first petition to exercise his calling in that town, and which, when finally set up, he was able to operate only three or four months, was sold in 1675 by his widow to John Foster, who had received permission from the licensers to open an office for printing in Boston.

John Foster was the son of Hopestill Foster, a prominent citizen of Dorchester, Massachusetts. He received his education from Harvard College, and obtained his bachelor's degree in 1667. After graduation he still remained at the College, pursuing a post-graduate course, but did not complete the course, as his name does not appear in the Quinquennial Catalogue among those who have taken the degree of Master of Arts. On June 8, 1669, the Rev. Hope Atherton, also a graduate of Harvard College, but at that time teaching the school in Dorchester, having accepted a call from the people of Hatfield to become their pastor, was granted permission by the town to terminate his engagement by September 29 following. John Foster was chosen as his successor, and is supposed to have commenced teaching the school in October. He probably intended to complete his post-graduate course, as in one of the

[3]

articles of his agreement with the town it was "granted as a liberty to the master, if he see it meet, for to go once in a fortnight to a lecture." His salary was £25 a year, but in 1670 was increased to £30. From recent investigations by Dr. Samuel A. Green, the eminent antiquary, it appears that Mr. Foster had a natural talent for drawing and sketching, and very early in his life became interested in wood-engraving. Having secured the proper tools, he probably employed his leisure hours in learning the art. From the crudeness of his printed work it is very probable that he was a self-taught artist, although he may have received hints from John Hull, the mint-master, and Edward Budd, a well-known carver who was in Boston as early as 1665. His first engraving is supposed to be the portrait of Rev. Richard Mather, who died April 22, 1669, and whose life, written by his son, Rev. Increase Mather, was published at Cambridge in 1670, "printed by S. G. and M. J." It was the first of Increase Mather's publications printed in New England, and one copy at least is known to have had as a frontispiece this cut. Three other copies of the portrait are known to be in existence, which do not appear to have been extracted from books, and the inference is that the portrait was engraved while Mr. Mather was living, by whom it was presented to his relatives and friends. Foster next found a practical use for his talent in his school work. In a letter to the Commissioners of the United Colonies dated September, 1671, Mr. Eliot writes : " Further I do present you with our Indians A B C and our Indian Dialogues with a request that you could pay printer's work. An ingenious young scholar (Sir Foster) did cut in wood the scheme, for which work I request that you would pay him. I think him worthy of 3 or 4 or 5 pounds but I leave it to your wisdoms." The use of the title " Sir" would indicate that the cutting had been done in 1670, while Foster was attending lectures, and before he had taken the Master's degree, which usually occurred three years after graduation. What this "scheme" was is a puzzle. A little light is obtained from Foster's agreement with the town of Dorchester. On December 23, 1672, it was agreed that Mr. Foster "shall teach such latin scholars as shall come to his father's house one whole year next ensuing from the first of January next, and to instruct and give out copies to such as come to him to learn to write, for his pains to have £10." Presumably Foster had been teaching privately at his own house such scholars as would come to him to write. The town now employed him as a public writing master at an advance in his salary of £10. Foster evidently had been using copy slips printed in script from wooden blocks on which he had engraved the letters of the alphabet, words and sentences. Undoubtedly these slips had been printed by Johnson, the Corporation printer, and had caught the attention of Mr. Eliot in his visits to Johnson's office. Impressed with the superiority of these copies over his own manuscript copies, and of the great saving in time in making copies, evidently he engaged Foster to devise a "scheme" which he could use in his Indian schools. One of the definitions of the word "scheme" is, "any lineal or mathematical diagram." It is possible that Foster designed a small chart to be hung up in the schoolroom, on which the characters written in Indian had been printed in script, from blocks engraved by him. The price, however, which he was to receive would seem to indicate that it was something more costly than a small chart or poster. The writer thinks that the "scheme" was more in the nature of a writing book, similar to the familiar writing book of our boyhood days, in the headlines of each page of which were printed in script, from engraved blocks, first slanting and curved lines, then the letters of the alphabet, and later words and sentences. The children had already been taught their letters and syllables from the hornbooks and common primers which Mr. Eliot had imported, but the copies in these writing books were to be in the Indian language, and from them the Indian children were to be taught to write and read the Indian language, and to them Eliot gave the name of "Indian A B C." As no copies of the "scheme" are in existence, every one has the privilege of conjecturing what it might have been. They were printed by Johnson. In the inventory of Johnson's stock we find "writing books" which probably were Foster's writing books in English. As the writing books in Indian would be printed only for Eliot's use, and would be paid for out of the Corporation stock, naturally no copies would be found in the inventory.

In 1672 Foster engraved on wood the Colonial seal, using as his model the original silver seal which was cut in England, and sent over to Governor Endicott in 1629. As in different editions of the Colonial Laws the engravings of this seal show variations, he must have cut it several times.

In 1677 Foster printed Rev. William Hubbard's *Narrative of the Troubles with the Indians*. It was accompanied by a *Map of New England*, undoubtedly engraved by Foster from a manuscript map drawn by Mr. Hubbard. It is known as the "Wine Hills" map, as the White Mountains are so designated on it. There were so many other errors in the lettering of the map, due probably to a faulty reading of Mr. Hubbard's manuscript, who lived so far away from the press that he was unable to correct the proof, that a second block was cut by Foster to accompany the edition of the *Narrative* which was printed in London a few months later. This corrected map is known as the "White Hills" map. In the London edition of the *Narrative* not only is the map corrected, but many errors in the text of the Boston edition also, as not one of the "Errata" which are noted on the last leaf of the Boston edition appears in the London edition.

Foster also showed his talent in drawing by sketching a view

of Boston as it appeared from East Boston.   In a letter to his
brother John Winthrop, Jr., at New London, Connecticut, dated
Boston, June 22, 1680, Wait Winthrop says: " I have sent you
a map of the town, with Charlestown, taken by Mr. Foster, the
printer, from Noddles Island.   Twas sent for Amsterdam, and
there printed." [1]   As this view was to be engraved on metal,
Foster was obliged to send it out of the country.   Messrs.
Dankers and Sluyter, two Dutch travellers, visited Boston in
1680.   They made many sketches of the different parts of the
country visited by them, and it may have been through their
recommendation that the sketch was sent to Amsterdam.   No
copy of this view is known to be in existence.   It is supposed
to be the prototype of what is known as Price's View of Boston.

Naturally Mather and Eliot became very much interested in
the young engraver, and were ready to help him in every way
possible.   The printing of his blocks brought him into close
contact with Green and Johnson, and he soon became interested
in printing.   He undoubtedly spent many hours watching the
workmen at their different tasks, and perhaps occasionally tried
his hand in setting type.   From a letter which we quote later it
appears that he was on more friendly terms with Johnson than
he was with Green, which is explained by the fact that Johnson
was a trained printer, and knew thoroughly every part of his
calling.   When Johnson died, presumably both Mather and
Eliot encouraged and urged Foster to continue the office.   It
was very desirable that the press should remain in Boston, and
it is therefore not surprising that he applied for and received
permission to operate " the press now set up in Boston."   He
was able, however, to buy only the press, as the types had already
been bought by Green, — that is, the font owned by Johnson.
Green had expected to secure the font belonging to the Corporation, which Johnson brought over, and which he had

[1] *Mass. Hist. Society Proceedings.*   Second Series, XVIII, 54.

previously made so many efforts to obtain. But Mr. Eliot controlled this font, and although Green hoped to secure it through the influence of Thomas Danforth, one of the Massachusetts Commissioners, yet Eliot, through the stronger influence of William Stoughton, also a Massachusetts Commissioner, was able to keep it and thus assure Foster both press and type. Green was so disappointed that he wrote the following very interesting letter[1] to John Winthrop, Jr., one of the Connecticut Commissioners, in which he gives a view of the condition of affairs as he saw it, together with a brief review of printing since 1649. It reads :

CAMBRIDGE, July 6 : 75.

Honoured Sir.

I make bold to present my service to your worship, as also to make known something of those aggrievances that I have met withal of late, entreating your worship's favor so far as your wisdom shall see fit. It is about printing; the employment I was called unto when there was none in the country to carry it along, after the death of him[2] that was brought over for that work by Mr. Jose Glover; and although I was not used unto it, yet being urged thereunto by one and another of place, did what by my own endeavours and help that I got from some others that was procured. I undertook the work and brought up my son to the same, and was employed in the Indian work, and the first that did anything that way, as I suppose your worship may remember; and so that Mr. Eliot was very glad of it, and it was a means as I suppose of promoting his interest; but when the Bible came to be printed, Mr. Eliot was desirous that it might be carried on with what expedition might be (and) was willing and desirous I should have help, whereupon it was thought convenient to send to the Corporation in England to

---

[1] *Mass. Hist. Soc'y Coll.* Fifth Series, I, 422–424.
[2] Matthew Day.

send one to be helpful in that work with me. By that means Mr. Johnson was sent over, and upon what terms and in what way your worship then knew, being one of the Commissioners; but after some time, he being subtle and somewhat prejudiced against me, because by my means he was disappointed of his intentions in marriage with my daughter, because he had a wife in London, he wound into favor with Mr. Eliot to work me out, that himself might get in, and when he went for England having letters from Mr. Eliot on his behalf, and was betrusted by the Honourable Corporation in London to bring over some letters that the Honoured Commissioners that met at Hartford that year (through my request) sent for, and with money he received from them brought over also letters for himself, and, with a little money more, a press also, so that when he came over again he was so high that I was not regarded, nor what I had formerly done. I was forced to comply with him to my great disadvantage to me and mine, and at last wrought me quite out of the Indian work and have been so ever since, which work is the most considerable of any work in the country because of the pay for it. But the overseers of the College sending to London to the Corporation (when they perceived how things went) to give to the College these letters that were theirs, the answering their desire partly that they should have the use of them until they saw reason to call for them again; but Mr. Johnson got Mr. Eliot to interpose that he might have them still in his hand until he could procure some for his use. He hath had them still in his hand, whereas the Corporation did send express order for the delivering of them, and that what was theirs might be together in the hands, and for the use of the College. Now it hath pleased God to take Mr. Johnson out of this world by death this last winter; and I would very fain and was desirous to have the letters, and I bought what was Mr. Johnson's, but Mr. Eliot through the help of Mr. Stoughton, one of the Commissioners for our Colony, put them into the hands of a young man that had no skill of printing but what he had taken notice by the by, and the Indian work is all put into his hand, and I and my son altogether defeated, although Mr. Danforth, the other of our Commissioners, gave me an order for the receiving of the letters belonging to the Corporation; but we are disappointed, and the work transmitted to others, from whom made the first onset, so that if your worship can do anything for our relief by writing to the Corporation at London I should account myself ever engaged more abundantly to your worship; and if something be not done that way I suppose the Corporation will also be disappointed, their letters spoiled, and estate wasted. I am very loath to be so troublesome to your worship, but I know no better way than to let your worship understand so far as I may. I hope your worship will pardon my boldness and shall leave it with your wisdom, not further to trouble your worship, but remain, as ever I have cause to do, Sir, your poor servant

SAMUEL GREEN."

Whether or not Winthrop took any notice of this letter does not appear, but apparently not, as the types still remained in Foster's office. From what Green says about Foster it is very evident that he had not a very high opinion of his abilities, and it does not appear probable that Foster had spent any time in his printing office in his younger days. Although it was true that Foster was "a young man that had no skill in printing but what he had taken notice by the way," yet this did not deter Foster, a bright young man, from accepting the responsibility, any more than it did Green himself twenty-five years before. Foster bought the press, employed skilful workmen, and using the Corporation types, published in June, 1675, the first book which bears in the imprint the name of Boston. It was a sermon by Increase Mather entitled *The Wicked Man's Portion*. A copy of this book at the Brinley sale in March, 1879, brought one hundred and fifty dollars. Another copy at the Hurst sale, in November, 1904, brought two hundred and fifty.

Green, however, was determined to get possession of that font of type. The College press was sadly in need of it, especially as the College had no funds to spare for the purchase of a new font. Accordingly, in June, 1677, a suit was entered in Court against the executor of Mrs. Johnson's will. The Middlesex County Court Records[1] contain the following entry:

"At a County Court held at Charlestown June 19, 1677, Mr. John Hayward attorney in behalf of the Commissioners of the United Colonies plaintiff, against Jonathan Cane, executor to the last will and testament of Ruth Johnson, administratrix to the estate of her husband Marmaduke Johnson deceased, in an action of the case for detaining a font of letters, bought by the said Johnson with money that he received for that end and use of the Honorable Corporation in London constituted by his Majesty for propagating of the gospel to the Indians in New England, and also for detaining a printer's chase, and other implements that belong to a printing press, and is appertaining to the said Indian stock, according to attachment dated 8, 4, 77. Both parties appeared and joined issue in the case. The jury having heard their respective pleas and evidence in the case, brought in their verdict, finding for the plaintiff that the defendant shall deliver the weight of letters expressed in the attachment, with other materials expressed in the attachment, or the value thereof in money, which we find to be forty pounds, with costs of court. The defendant made his appeal to the next Court of Assistants."

The appeal was not successful, as, in the record of a Court of Assistants held at Boston September 4, 1677, is the following entry:

[1] Vol. III, p. 176.

"Jonathan Cane executor to the last will of Ruth Johnson administratrix to the estate of Marmaduke Johnson deceased plaintiff against John Hayward attorney in behalf of the Commissioners of the United Colonies defendant in an action of appeal from the judgment of the County Court at Charlestown in June last after the attachment and evidence in the case, Court's Judgment, reason of appeal, &c, were read, committed to the jury, and are remaining on file with the Records of this Court, the jury brought in their verdict. They found for the defendant confirmation of the former judgment and cost of Courts thirty seven shillings and eight pence."

The font probably was given up, as in 1678 Foster had procured a new font of long primer, after which he produced much handsomer books than he had been able to do with the Corporation font.

Foster was a bookseller as well as a printer and an engraver, and also compiled an almanac annually. His shop, according to the imprint of *A Brief History of the Wars with the Indians in New England. By Increase Mather*, printed in 1676, was *over against* the *Sign of the Dove*. The Hotel Touraine occupies very nearly its site, as the *Sign of the Dove* was the sign attached to an inn on the corner of Snow's Lane and a "lane leading from the Common," of which Captain William Wright was landlord. The Masonic Temple occupies the site of the Dove Tavern. At that time the "lane leading from the Common," now Tremont Street, did not cross Snow's Lane, now Boylston Street.

Foster died of consumption, after a long illness, on September 9, 1681, aged thirty-two years. In his will dated July 18, 1681, he directs "What I have in Boston belonging to printing may be sold and such debts as are due in Boston may be paid therewith." He also bequeaths twenty shillings apiece to Rev. John Eliot of Roxbury, Rev. Increase Mather, and Mr. Cotton

THE
NECESSITY

OF

The pouring out of the Spirit from on High

UPON A

Sinning Apostatizing People, set under Judgment, in order to their merciful Deliverance and Salvation.

As it was Delivered in part, upon 21. 9. 1678. being a general FAST throughout the united Colonies of *N.E.*

By WILLIAM ADAMS,
Pastor of the Church of Christ in *Dedham.*

Luk. 19. 41, 42. *And when he was come near, he beheld the City and wept over it, saying, If thou hadst known even then, at least in this thy day, the things which belong unto thy peace ! but now they are hid from thine eyes.*

Luk. 13. 35. *Behold, your house is left unto you desolate. And verily I say unto you, Ye sha'll not see me, until the time come when ye shall say, Blessed is he that cometh in the Name of the Lord.*

Psal. 14. 7. *O that the Salvation of Israel were come out of Sion ! when the Lord bringeth back the Captivity of his People, Jacob shall rejoice and Israel shall be glad.*

BOSTON;
Printed by *John Foster,* for *William Avery,* near the sign of the blew Anchor. 1679.

Mather of Boston. In the inventory of his estate, which was appraised at £106 13s. 6d., the printing office was appraised at £60.

Many other facts regarding John Foster have been brought to light by the investigations of that careful observer Samuel Abbott Green, LL.D., Vice-President of the Massachusetts Historical Society, which he has recorded in *Ten Fac-simile Reproductions relating to Old Boston and Neighborhood*, published in 1901, and in *Proceedings of the Massachusetts Historical Society*, Second Series, Vol. XVIII, published in 1905. The writer has devoted several pages to the career of John Foster as a bookseller in *Early Boston Booksellers* published by the Club of Odd Volumes in 1900. To all of these books the reader is respectfully referred.

Samuel Sewall

Samuel Sewall

THE death of John Foster again endangered the existence of the press in Boston, and those who were most interested in its continuance immediately sought for some person who would be competent and willing to undertake its management. Their choice fell upon Samuel Sewall, the son of Henry and Alice (Dummer) Sewall of Newbury, Mass. He was born at Horton, England, March 28, 1652, during the temporary residence of his parents there. He entered Harvard College in 1667, receiving his degree of Bachelor of Arts in 1671, and Master of Arts in 1674. He was chosen Tutor of the College in 1673, and in 1674 was appointed " Keeper of the College Library." He studied divinity and occasionally preached; but having married, February 28, 1675–6, the daughter of John Hull, mint-master and treasurer of the Colony, he retired from the ministry and sought for some position in mercantile life. For a few years he went among the merchants and tried to familiarize himself with business pursuits. In 1680 he accepted a business account and sold a consignment of glasses and hats on commission. His success in the commission business, and his possession of capital, recommended him to Rev. Increase Mather, Rev. Samuel Willard, Rev. Samuel Torrey, and others, who were interested in the Boston press, and they offered him the position of manager. To be the manager of the press evidently was more attractive than to be a commission merchant, so Sewall accepted, and within six months of the death of Foster had published *Ne Sutor ultra Crepidam. Or brief Animadversions upon the New-England Ana-*

baptists late fallacious Narrative; wherein the Notorious Mistakes and Falsehoods by them Published, are Detected. By Samuel Willard Teacher of a Church in Boston in New England. Boston in New-England, Printed by S. Green upon Assignment of S. Sewall. And are to be Sold by Sam. Phillips, at the Westend of the Exchange, 1681.

It is a small quarto of thirty-five pages, and when sold at the Brinley sale brought twenty-nine dollars. On the upper margin of the title-page of a copy of this book in the library of the Massachusetts Historical Society is written, " And^r Belcher the Gift of Mr. Sam^{ll} Greene Decr 168[ ]."

This probably is the second publication under Sewall's management, and the imprint shows that as he knew nothing about the mechanical part of the business, he had secured the services of Samuel Green, Jr., of New London, Connecticut, a skilful printer, who seems to have followed Johnson's example in stipulating that his name should appear in the imprints. The first publication under Sewall's management presumably is: *An Ephemeris of Coelestial Motions, Aspects, Eclipses, etc. For the Year of the Christian Aera 1682. By W. Brattle Philomath. Cambridge Printed by Samuel Green 1682.* On the title-page of a copy of this almanac, which formerly belonged to Sewall but now in the library of the Massachusetts Historical Society, is written " Ex dono Authoris Jan^r. 30. 1681." On the last page is written : " The last half Sheet was Printed wth my Letters at Boston. S.S." The almanac contains twenty-four pages, sixteen of which are in one kind of type and eight in another. This is explained by Mr. Sewall's note, by which it appears that sixteen pages were printed in Cambridge and eight in Boston.[1] The presentation inscription shows that it must have been printed previous to January 30, 1681–2.

Whether or not Sewall bought the Foster press does not

---

[1] Samuel Green, Jr., arrived in Boston in December, 1681.

appear, but probably he did not. "Printed with my Letters" meant that the types were in his possession as manager.

The license to print granted by the General Court does not indicate ownership. The record of the license as it appears in the *Records of the Governor and Company of the Massachusetts Bay in New England* reads:

" 1681 Oct. 12. Mr. Samuel Sewall, at the instance of some friends, with respect to the accommodations of the public, being prevailed with to undertake the management of the printing press in Boston, late under the improvement of Mr. John Foster, deceased, liberty is accordingly granted to him for the same by this Court, and none may presume to set up any other press without the like liberty first granted."

This would seem to indicate that several gentlemen, interested in keeping the press in Boston, had joined together, purchased the office, and persuaded Sewall to manage it. Probably they had taken the office with all its engagements just as Foster left it, and made no change in the location, which was only a short distance from Sewall's residence. At the end of the Preface of a book printed in 1682 appears in print the following notice: " This insuing Discourse had been Printed sooner, had not Mr. John Foster (the Printer) been disenabled by a tedious sickness of which he died."

Sewall continued as manager until the latter part of 1683, as on October 16, 1683, the General Court ordered the treasurer to pay him for printing Mr. Torrey's Election Sermon for that year. During his two years of management Sewall published twenty or more books, a goodly showing, among the best known of which is *Heaven's Alarm to the World. By Increase Mather. The Second Impression. Boston, 1682.* The first impression had been printed by John Foster in 1681. All the copies of the second impression which were not sold, in 1683 were bound with another sermon by Increase Mather on the same subject, which had been preached later, to which a general title-page was prefixed, which reads in part:

ΚΟΜΗΤΟΓΡΑΙΦΑ. *Or a Discourse Concerning Comets: wherein the Nature of Blazing Stars is Enquired into. . . . As also two Sermons Occasioned by the late Blazing Stars. By Increase Mather, Teacher of a Church at Boston in New England. Boston in New England. Printed by S. G. for S. S. And sold by J. Browning at the corner of Prison Lane next the Town-House. 1683.*

On October 1, 1683, John Hull, the father-in-law of Sewall, died, and there was soon published a book entitled, *The High Esteem which God hath of the Death of his Saints. As it was Delivered in a Sermon Preached October 7, 1683. Occasioned by the Death of the Worshipful John Hull Esq. Who Deceased October 1, 1683. By Samuel Willard Teacher of a Church in Boston. Boston in New England. Printed by Samuel Green for Samuel Sewall: 1683.* On the last two pages is a Latin Elegy " in obitum . . . Johannis Hull, Armigeri," by Elijah Corlet.

It is a small quarto of twenty-two pages, and when sold in the Brinley sale brought seventeen dollars and fifty cents. This probably was the last book printed under the management of Sewall. Hull had left a large estate, the care of which falling upon Sewall would cause him to wish to be relieved of the responsibility of the management of the press. On November 7, 1683, he was elected Deputy to the General Court by the town of Westfield, which office had been held by his father-in-law in 1671–1673, and in 1684 was chosen one of the Assistants, succeeding his father-in-law, who had held that office from 1680 until his death.

As no book later than Willard's Sermon on the death of John Hull has been found with the name of Sewall in the imprint it is presumed that he retired from the management of the press about this time. The following entry is taken from the *Records of the Governor and Company of the Massachusetts Bay in New England:*

HEAVEN'S
ALARM
TO THE
WORLD.
OR

A SERMON, wherein is shewed,
That Fearful

Sights

And Signs in Heaven, are the *PRESA-*
GES of great *CALAMITIES* at hand.
Preached at the Lecture of Boston in New-England,
January, 20. 1680.

By Mr. *INCREASE MATHER.*

The Second *IMPRESSION.*

Rev. 8. 10. *And the third Angel sounded, and there fell*
a great Star from heaven, burning as it were a Lamp, &c.
Rev. 11. 14. —— *behold, the third Wo cometh quickly.*

BOSTON IN NEW-ENGLAND,
Printed for *Samuel Sewall.* And are to be sold by
John Brown ng at the Corner of the *Prison-Lane*
Next the Town-House. 1682.

" Whereas, at a session of the General Court in October 1681, this Court was pleased to intrust Mr. Samuel Sewall with the management of the printing press in Boston, lately under the improvement of Mr. John Foster, deceased, and whereas, by the providence of God, Mr. Samuel Sewall is rendered unable to attend the same, he judging it reasonable to acquaint this honoured Court therewith, desiring that he may be freed from any obligation unto respecting that affair, with thankful acknowledgements of the liberty then granted, . . .

" The Court grants the request above mentioned."

This would seem to indicate that Sewall had no ownership of the press, and that he wished to magnify the importance of the office by having it appear that it was an official appointment. As a matter of business it was unnecessary. Samuel Green, Jr., had continued with Sewall during the whole time of his management, and when Sewall retired took his place. In his Diary Sewall says but very little about his experiences as a tradesman or a printer, and when the office which he had managed was destroyed by fire he does not mention it, although he speaks of other buildings destroyed in the same fire.

Samuel Green, Jr.

Samuel Green, Jr.

THE imprint of *The Boston Ephemeris. An Almanack for the Year MDCLXXXIV. By Benjamin Gillam, Philonauticus* reads *Boston in New England, Printed by Samuel Green for Samuel Phillips, and are to be Sold at his Shop at the West end of the Town-House. 1684.* The rival almanac entitled *Cambridge Ephemeris. . . . By N. Russel, Astrotyr.* was printed by the father of Samuel Green, Jr., at Cambridge. In Noadiah Russell's Diary[1] are the following entries: "12th 11. (1683) I went to Cambridge to carry my Almanack to ye Press. 26 11 (1684)[2] My Almanack was printed." It is very probable that Benjamin Gillam gave the manuscript of his almanac to Samuel Green, Jr., at about the same time. As Samuel Green's name is not associated with Sewall's in the imprint, nor does Sewall's name appear again in the imprints, it would seem to be very probable that, although Sewall was not officially released from the management of the press until September 12, 1684, yet in reality the actual management of the press certainly, as early as March, 1684, was in the hands of Samuel Green, Jr., and possibly since Sewall's election to the General Court on November 7, 1683.

Samuel Green, Jr., was the son of the well-known Cambridge printer, Samuel Green, and was born in Cambridge March 16, 1648. He was brought up by his father as a printer, with whom he worked as late as 1675, about which time he removed to Hartford and later to New London. Before 1677 he had

---

[1] *New England Historical and Genealogical Register*, VII, 59.
[2] Error for 1683.

married Hannah Butler, daughter of Deacon Richard Butler of
Hartford. Richard Butler was one of the early settlers of
Cambridge, but removed to Hartford with Hooker. He died
August 6, 1684, and in his will dated April 2, 1677, among
other bequests he gives to his daughters Mary Wright, Elizabeth Olmsted, and Hannah Green, twenty shillings apiece. It
is very probable that it was through the financial assistance of
his father-in-law that Samuel Green was able to assume the
management of the press when, late in 1683, Samuel Sewall
wished to be released from it. He returned to Boston at the
request of Sewall, who, according to the Town Records, on
December 26, 1681, became surety that "Samuel Green or his
family should not become chargeable to the Town."

Although Samuel Green, Jr., was the real manager of the
press in 1684, yet he did not receive his license until May,
1685. The following petition, taken from Massachusetts Ar-
chives, Vol. 58, p. 135, furnishes many interesting facts about
Samuel Green, Jr.

"To the Honorable General Court, now assembled together
in Boston, the humble petition of Samuel Green printer humbly
sheweth to your honors, That whereas Mr. Samuel Sewall was
ready and willing for the public good to undertake the management of the printing press, and in order thereto for his better
encouragement the honored General Court upon the 12th of
October in the year of our Lord 1681 did see meet to confirm
unto him the whole privilege thereof, and withal did order that
none might set up any other press in Boston without the like
liberty. Now may it please your honors seeing God by his
providence hath so ordered it to call unto himself Captain John
Hull the honored father-in-law of Mr. Samuel Sewall, and
since which time the aforesaid Mr. Sewall was called into a place
of public trust and other concerns, so that he cannot prosecute

his design as to the printing work. Your humble petitioner in obedience to his honored father left his habitation where he then was being in New London in the Colony of Connecticut and then in a convenient way of trading, which by God's blessing he was in a very comfortable way of living, yet was as willing and ready as well for the public good as his own interest and did remove himself and family out of the aforesaid Colony to Boston, since which time he hath been assisting to the abovesaid Mr. Sewall. Also since the aforesaid Mr. Sewall hath left off the improvement of the printing press, your humble petitioner hath laid out large sums of money in purchasing of several instruments and tools for the further improving and promoting of printing, whereby he hath straightened himself and family, hoping thereby to obtain to the same encouragement, liberty and license which is granted to Mr. Sewall. I humble request your honors to take it into your serious consideration, that I am a poor man, and that I have several young children, and the greatest part of the estate that I have is laid out in tools and instruments as abovesaid. And since your poor petitioner did enter upon the work of printing, which is about twenty years ago, and he having no other calling to betake himself unto whereby he may maintain himself and family, so hoping this honored General Court upon their prudent consideration of the premises will see just cause to grant your humble supplicant his request herein which will be for the promotion of the public good as well as my benefit. In which work I hope your honors shall find him readier in doing than saying, to the uttermost of his skill, in case your honors will be pleased to grant your humble petitioner a license and confirm it with as large liberties for printing, as your honors did to Mr. Sewall, all which being done by the honored General Court, for your petitioner shall engage, and as in duty he is bound, for the continuance of your honors long life with prosperity and everlasting happiness ever shall pray, so he is your honors humble supplicant in all dutiful submission, and your most humble servant

SAMUEL GREEN.

Boston the 7th of
MAY 1685."

What answer was made to this petition does not appear. Green, however, did not secure the exclusive right to print, but was obliged to share with Richard Pierce. Neither is it probable that he bought the press, as in the above petition he speaks of " instruments and tools for the further improving and promoting of printing." It presumably remained in the possession of the same parties who had induced Sewall to manage it, and who now promoted Green to that responsible position. For the first two or three years he is supposed to have remained in the same building which had been hired by Foster and Sewall, but from the Tax List of 1687 we find that he had moved to the south side of Milk Street. The imprint of *An Almanack for the Year of our Lord MDCLXXXIX* reads *Boston, Printed by Samuel Green, and are to be sold at his house over against the South-Meeting-House. 1689.*

John Dunton, the well-known London bookseller who arrived in Boston in March, 1686, and spent several months there and in the neighborhood, passed some of his leisure hours at the house of Green. In his *Life and Errors*, published in 1705, he gives Mr. Green and his wife very excellent characters. In speaking of Mrs. Green as a mother he says :

" As she is a good wife to her husband, so is she also a good mother to her children, whom she brings up with that sweetness and facility as is admirable not keeping them at too great a distance, as some do, thereby discouraging their good parts ; nor by over-fondness (a fault most mothers are guilty of) betraying them into a thousand inconveniences, which oftentimes proves fatal to them. In brief she takes care of their education, and

A PLEA

For the Life of

Dying Religion

from the Word of the Lord:

IN A

SERMON

Preached to the *GENERAL ASSEMBLY* of the
COLONY of the *MASSACHUSETS* at *Boston in
New-England*, May 16. 1 6 8 3.

Being the Day of *ELECTION* there.

By Mr. *Samuel Torrey* Pastor of the Church of Christ
at *Waymouth.*

Rev. 3. 1. *I know thy works that thou hast a name, that thou livest
and art dead.* 2. *Be watchful and strengthen the things
which remain, which are ready to dye.*

Deut. 30. 19. *I call heaven and earth to Record this day against
you that I have set before you life and death, blessing and cursing,
therefore chuse life that both thou and thy seed may live.* 20 *That
thou mayest love the Lord thy God, and that thou mayest obey his
voice, and that thou mayest cleave to him, for he is thy life.*

Hosea 6. 1. *Come let us return to the Lord.*——— 2 *After two
dayes he will revive us, and in the third day he will raise us up,
and we shall live in his sight.*

BOSTON IN NEW-ENGLAND

Printed by *Samuel Green* for *Samuel Sewall.* 1683.

whatever else belongs to them, so that Mr. Green enjoys the comfort of his children, without knowing anything of the trouble of them."

In speaking of Mr. Green he says:

" The next was Mr. Green, a printer. I contracted a great friendship with this man. To name his trade will convince the world he was a man of good sense and understanding. He was so facetious and obliging in his conversation, that I took a great delight in his company and made use of his house to while away my melancholy."

Green managed the press very successfully, printing between 1685 and 1690 inclusive fifty or more books. In 1687 he had as an assistant his brother Bartholomew, then twenty-one years of age. One of the last books printed by Samuel Green was *The Present State of New England. By Cotton Mather. Boston. Printed by Samuel Green. 1690.* It is a small duodecimo of fifty-four pages, and at the sale of the library of Bishop Hurst, November 28, 1904, a copy brought two hundred and ninety dollars. The sermon was preached March 20, 1690, on account of the war with the French, our first Intercolonial War. The preacher spoke freely of the condition of affairs in New England, and tells the people that their own dissensions were the cause of the invasion. He says:

" You are those that every Day do the things, *For which the Wrath of God comes.* This people of God is now in such *Distress* and *Danger* as it never saw before; and I ask not your leave to tell you, *That you are the Authors of it all.* Tis You that bring whole Armyes of *Indians* and *Gallic* Blood Hounds in upon us; tis *you* that clog all our *Councels* with such Delay and Slowness, as terrifies us in our most Rational Expectations. You are perhaps the most Querimonious and Outragious of all People in your *Discontents.*"

After telling the people of their iniquities he says:

"The last Evening filled us with new Alarms of an Attack from New France upon this poor land; which was before involved in Calamities that astonished us. . . . Wherefore I take leave to *mind* you, of what, I suppose every man can *Tell* me. . . . *We are in great Distress.* . . . This may I truly say, *He is no New Englander* (not worthy of the Name) *who at such a Time as this, will not Venture his All, for this Afflicted people of God.* . . . We have at this time a great Service to be done for their Majesties: K. William, and Q. Mary, whom God grant long to Reign ; and this not *only* by Securing their Interest in *this* large Territory, and Consequently in all *America*, but *also* by making a brisk Salley forth upon the French Territories, which must else be a Perpetual obstacle to the Thriving of these Plantations."

The Proclamation at the end urges the people to abstain from all evil doing. " That the Towns within this Jurisdiction take special care to avoid *Factions* and *Quarrels* in their *Town Affairs ;* that God may bless them in the war."

This Proclamation had been ordered by the General Court on March 13, 1690, and was printed as a broadside by Green on March 17. During the next three months he printed commissions for officers; on March 24 a broadside " about Sr : William (Phips) to go General"; on June 20 " a Proclamation for Souldiers to go against Canada," and on June 30 a Proclamation for a fast.

Mrs. Green died July 16, 1690, a few days before her husband, both of small-pox, which dreadful disease visited Boston in that year and carried off a large number of the inhabitants. His brother Bartholomew continued the office in the interest of the estate, but on the night of September 16 the building which contained the office was partially destroyed by fire. The single number of *Public Occurrences* published on September 25, 1690, refers to the fire as follows:

The Present State of New-England.

Confidered in a

DISCOURSE

On the Neceffities and Advantages of a

Public Spirit

In every *MAN*;

Efpecially, At fuch a time as this.

Made at the LECTURE in *Bofton*
20. d. 1. m. 1690:

Upon the News of an Invafion by bloody
INDIANS and FRENCH-MEN, begun
upon Us.

By Cotton Mather.

——Non difplicuiffe meretur,
Feftinat Patriæ qui placuiffe fuæ.

BOSTON

Printed by Samuel Green. 1690.

" Between the sixteenth and seventeenth of this instant another Fire broke forth near the South-Meeting-House which consumed about five or six houses and had almost carried the Meeting-House itself, one of the fairest edifices in the country, if God had not remarkably assisted the Endeavours of the People to put out the Fire. . . . There were two more considerable Circumstances in the Calamities of this Fire, one was that a young man belonging to the House where the Fire began, unhappily perished in the Flames. . . . Another was that the best furnished PRINTING PRESS, of those few we know of in America was lost ; a loss not presently to be repaired."

In his *Diary* Sewall makes the following record :

" Tuesday, Sept. 16. About eleven at night a fire broke out at the house of Jno. Allen, worsted comber, in which his apprentice, Sam. Worster was burned with the house of Lieutenant Reynolds, Mr. Bligh, Langden and a great part of Savel Simsons. The wind being southwest, the South-Meeting-House was preserved with very much difficulty, being in a flame in divers places of it. Captain Cyprian Southack and Lieut. David Mason did very worthily hazarding themselves with many others on the Lead for a great while."

Singularly enough Sewall does not refer to the destruction of the printing office which he had managed only six years previously. The fire began in the house of John Allen, which was situated nearly opposite the present Bromfield Street, and driven by a southwest wind swept towards the Old South Meeting House, destroying all the houses on the easterly side of Washington Street in the following order, viz. John Langdon, Thomas Bligh, John Lake, Lieutenant Reynolds, and Savil Simpson. Lieutenant Reynolds' house was built of stone, and occupied the south corner of Washington and Milk streets. This stone building, although itself destroyed, saved the meeting-house. Passing down Milk Street the next house was Savil Simpson's, which was partly burned, and where the fire was stopped. Savil Simpson's house, probably, was the house occupied by Green, both as a printing office and as a residence. We learn from the inventory of his estate, which was not taken until after the fire, that some of his household goods were saved, and as this was the only house which was partially burned, it must have been the home of the press which unfortunately was burned.

The inventory of Mr. Green's estate is on file at the office of the Registrar of Probate for Suffolk County, Massachusetts, of which we present an official copy.

Inventory of yᵉ estate of m Samuel Green late of Boston, Deceased: taken Since the late Fire and Appraised pr us whose Names are under written october 10th 1690.

	℔	s	_
Impʳⁱᵉ a pr of Shooebuckles and a Sett of Silver Shirt Buttons	00	08	00
Item a Red Trunk 4s. & 3 Small bookes 15d & 4old Razors 2s	00	07	03
tt A Knife 3d and a Ivory-headed Cane 2s	00	02	03
tt A looking glass 23s & A Silver Cup 3℔	04	03	00
tt A Carbine 10s and a brass Sconce 4s	00	14	00
tt A Small looking-glass 1s & a ～～ erence-wine bottle 4d	00	01	04
tt A Glass-Case 4s and an old Round Table 1s	00	05	00
tt A Square table 8s & 6 leather Cheares at 6s pr chear	02	04	00
tt 6 old Ditto at 3s pr chear, 18s and 3 Ditto flagg cheares 2s : 4d	01	00	04
tt An old pr of Andirons 3s & 3 old Spoons	00	03	04
tt A Small black Table	00	03	00
tt 2 baggs of New Cloth 6s & a Chest of Drawer of Japan work 35s	02	01	00
tt A Dressing Box of Japan Work	00	15	00
tt 4 Turky-work Cheares at 8s & 2 old Ditto Stools at 2s	01	16	00

	℔	s	d
tt A pr of Mony Scales 2s. 6d. & A half-hour glass 6d.	00	03	00
tt An old pr of Bellows 6d & a Comb-Case 3	00	00	09
tt 10 doz : of Psalters at 9s pr Doz	04	10	00
tt 46 Doz : & 4 larger Catechisms at 3s pr Doz :	06	19	00
tt 06 Doz of Smaller Ditto at 18d pr Doz :	00	09	00
tt 14 Bookes 10s & Wast paper	00	10	09
tt an old feather bed qt 73lb at 10d pr lb	03	00	10
tt 2 Bolsters, a pillow & A feather bed qt 67 lb at 12d	03	07	00
tt 50lb of Pewter at 12d pr lb	02	10	00
tt 43–½ of Flax at 6d & a Small pcel of Damag'd Ditto	01	02	09
tt A Iron pott & hooks 5s and 3 Small Kettles 10s	00	15	00
tt A pr of Brass Scales 4s & a 2 pound Weight, 6d	00	04	06
tt A brass fender, and a pr of Andirons	00	10	00
tt An old Tester 1s & an oval box 1s & 2 Images 4d	00	02	04
tt A large Worsted Rugg 28s and Small Trunk 8d	01	08	08
tt an old Rugg 7s & A Coverlid 18s	01	05	00
tt an old Ditto 8s & A blankett 4s & an old Ditto 18d	00	13	06
tt A Cotten Coverlid 7s Silk Curtaines & Valens 18s	01	05	00
tt A pr of Serge Curtaines 26s 8 pr of green Ditto 10s	01	16	00
tt A Counterpaine of flowered Callico 18s	00	18	00
tt A Callico Carpett	00	06	00
tt A Cloke 20s & a Silk Wastcoat 18s	01	18	00
tt A black & Serge breeches	04	10	00
tt A Corse broad-Cloth Coat & Breeches	02	01	00
tt A pr of plush breeches, & Serge Coate	02	05	00
tt a Serge Wastcoat 6s & a pr of old Breeches 1s	00	07	00
tt A pr of white curtains & lac'd Valens	01	02	00
tt A pr of Window Curtains 6s & a holland Cup-board Cloth 5s	00	11	00
tt 2 pr of Brown Sheets	00	14	00
Nᵒ 1 tt A pr Ditto 10s	00	10	00
9 tt A pr Ditto 4s	00	04	00
12 tt A pr Ditto 5s	00	05	00

	₶	s	d
17 tt a pr Ditto 15s	00	15	00
11 tt A pr Ditto 5s	00	05	00
8 tt A pr Ditto 7s	00	07	00
10 tt A pr Ditto 4s	00	04	00
7 tt A pr Ditto 3	00	03	00
2 tt A pr Ditto 2s	00	02	00
14 tt A pr Ditto 3s	00	03	00
22 tt one fine Ditto 9s	00	09	00
23 tt A pr Ditto 8s	00	08	00
5 tt A pr Ditto 7s	00	07	00
46 tt A pr Ditto 7s	00	07	00
30 tt one Small Ditto	00	02	09
37 tt A pr Ditto 8s	00	08	00
tt 3 pr Pillow beares — old	00	04	00
tt 9 Dieper Naptkins 8d pr Napt. 6s & A Diep table cloth 3s : 6d	00	09	06
tt 2 Stript Silk Crape Mantos	01	16	00
tt fringe for A peticoat, 1s & A Small Manto 5s	00	06	00
tt A pr of worsted Stockins	00	04	06
tt a pr of yarn Stockins 1s & one pr Silk Ditto 18d	00	02	06
tt a pr of tann'd gloves 3d & a Doz & halfe Button 9d	00	01	00
tt an old Sea-handkerchief 3d & a Stript-fashion Wastcoat 3s	00	03	03
tt 3 Neckcloths 4s one old Ditto & 2 Cravatts 18d	00	05	06
tt a pr of holland Sleeves 4s and a pr Small Ditto 1s	00	05	00
tt A Shirt 4s and an old Ditto : 1s	00	05	00
tt 2 Scotch cloth Shirts	00	09	00
tt 5 corse Naptkins 2s & 2 old Ditto 8d	00	02	08
tt 2 pr of yarn Stockins & one Single Ditto	00	03	06
tt 7 Stomachers 3s—6d and a prcell of Needles 1s	00	04	06
	69	10	03
Item 10 yards of Narrow fillitting at 1d pr yr	00	00	10
tt A yard & ½ of Bone Lace 3s: 2d & 6—½ yds Ditto at 18d pr yd	00	12	11
tt 8 yards & ¼ of Ditto at 10d pr yard	00	06	10

	ħb	s	d
tt A Wainscott Chest	oo	03	06
tt A Leaf of A table	oo	02	oo
tt A Candle-box	oo	oo	06
tt A Iron Curtain-Rod	oo	o1	06
tt Wast paper	oo	oo	06
tt 2 Brass Skilletts & A Brass Beasting Ladle	oo	06	oo
tt A Brass Kettle qt about 9 gallons	oo	17	oo
tt 9 bound Books	oo	05	oo
tt A Pillion and Pillion Cloth — old	oo	03	06
tt 3 Trunks of Women Apparel	21	oo	oo
tt Cash found in ye house	61	06	oo
tt 179 Bushells of Indian Corn at 2s pr Bushell	17	18	oo
tt 2 hogsds of Sugar qt about 18 et: o qr: oolb			
— at 17s pr et	15	06	oo
tt A list of Debts	123	14	11
	239	15	oo
	o69	10	03
Summa totalis	309	05	03

The Deceased, mr Samuel Green hath written y° following words at y° end of his List of Debts; vizt:

Divers other Small Debts in my Books wch w^re good looking after may be got.

I have a Stock of Cattle at one David Caulkins house at New London, I delivered one Cow, one Heifer, one Cow-Calfe which Stock to be delivered to me or mine and half the Increase: Now it is going on for 4 years.

I have leste   of land in   woods it may do some good in Time.

           JOHN MARION Senor
           RICHARD PIERCE
           JOHN ALLEN

BOSTON November 27th 1690

       made Oath in County Court that this is a Just and true Inventory of the Estate of the late Samuel Green Dec.^d

So farre as is Come to his knowledge and that when he knowes more he will cause it to be added

attest^r Joseph Webb   Clerk

Boston Novr 27. 1690

Copy Attest
Eugene Tappan
Ass't Register.

Two of the appraisers, Richard Pierce and John Allen, were brother printers. In the inventory no mention is made of ownership of house, printing press, or types, which is accounted for by the fact that, as has been shown, the house belonged to Savil Simpson, and the press to a company of gentlemen interested in keeping a printing office in Boston. We know, however, that Green had bought certain "tools and instruments for the improvements of the press." Some of these "tools and instruments" were undoubtedly types, as under the imprint of a catalogue of *The Library of the Late Reverend and Learned Mr. Samuel Lee*, printed in Boston in 1693, Rev. Thomas Prince has written: "Mr. B. Green says — This was Prind by his Broth Samuel's Letter, in Boston." Evidently some of the types had been saved from the fire, and as they were comparatively new, probably had been bought for the use of the Cambridge press, which was in great need of new type. Therefore the type would figure in the inventory only as cash. The listing of a pair of brass scales, 37 pairs of brown sheets, 179 bushels of Indian corn, and two hogsheads of sugar would indicate that, in addition to the printing office, Samuel Green was doing in Boston what he had been doing in New London, — namely, operating a general store.

Samuel Green had several children, some born in New London, and at least two in Boston. All are supposed to have died young, with the exception of a daughter, Mary, who is said to have married John Kneeland, Jr.

James Glen

A REFERENCE to the title-pages of a few books printed in the years 1682 and 1683 will show that Samuel Green, Jr., was not the only printer whose services were employed by Samuel Sewall while managing the press in Boston. The title-page of one of these volumes reads: *Covenant-Keeping the Way to Blessedness, or a brief Discourse wherein is shewn the Connexion which there is between the Promise, on God's Part; and Duty on Our Part, in the Covenant of Grace; as it was Delivered in several Sermons, preached in Order to Solemn Renewing of Covenant. By Samuel Willard, Teacher of a Church in Boston in New England. Boston in New England, printed by James Glen for Samuel Sewall, 1682.* Undoubtedly James Glen was the person recorded by Wyman in *The Genealogies and Estates of Charlestown* as " James Glenn of ketch ' Mary and Elizabeth ' from Scotland 1679." No other information concerning him is given. Although residing in Charlestown, presumably he found employment with John Foster and had charge of the printing office during his " tedious sickness." Possibly he may have been retained by the gentlemen interested in keeping the press in Boston to watch over the press and printing material until a manager could be found. Samuel Sewall was granted a license to print by the General Court, October 12, 1681. By advice of Samuel Green, the Cambridge printer, Sewall sent to Samuel Green, Jr., who was then residing in New London, Connecticut, an invitation to come to Boston and assist him in operating the press. The invitation was accepted, and Green arrived in Boston shortly

[39]

before December 26, 1681. Although there are indications that at the death of Foster the press was in full operation and manuscripts were in hand ready to be printed, yet apparently nothing was printed until after the arrival of Green.

When the name of James Glen first appeared in the imprints is unknown. It is possible that he printed the last eight pages of the *Almanac for 1682*, although neither his name nor that of Samuel Green, Jr., appears in the imprint. James Glen's name appears in the imprints of a few books printed during the years 1682 and 1683, but in none after the retirement of Sewall in the latter part of 1683. Thomas, in his *History of Printing in America*, says of him : " He printed under Sewall less than two years. I have seen only three or four works which bear his name in the imprint, and these were printed for Sewall."

What became of Glen is unknown. He may have been a competitor with Green for the license to print, and when that was secured by Green, preferred to be employed in the office of the young printer Richard Pierce.

Covenant-Keeping
The Way to
BLESSEDNESS
OR
A brief Difcourfe wherein is fhewn the
Connexion which there is between the
PROMISE, on *God's* Part,
and *DUTY*, on *Our* Part,

in the Covenant of Grace :

*As it was Delivered in feveral Sermons
Preached in Order to Solemn Renewing of*

Covenant.

By *SAMUEL WILLARD* Teacher
of a Church in *Bofton* in *New-England.*

Deut. 7. 9, *Know therefore that the Lord thy God, be
it God, the faithful God, which keepeth Covenant and.
Mercy with them that Love him, and keep his Commandments, to a thoufand Generations:*
10 *And repayeth them that Hate him, to their face, to de-
ftroy them: He will not be flack to him that hateth
Him, He will repay him to his face.*

BOSTON IN NEW-ENGLAND,
Printed by *James Glen,* for *Samuel Sewall.* 1682

Richard Pierce

Richard Pierce

OF the early life of Richard Pierce, the printer of *A Monumental Memorial*, nothing has been discovered. Thomas, in the *History of Printing in America*, says, " There was a printer in London by the name of Richard Pierce in 1679; and it is not improbable that he emigrated to this country and set up his press in Boston." An examination of what is known of Richard Pierce would seem to show that this supposition is not well founded.

On August 27, 1680, Richard Pierce, a printer of Boston, married Sarah Cotton, daughter of the Rev. Seaborn Cotton, of Hampton, New Hampshire, who was the eldest son of the Rev. John Cotton of Boston. Through his mother, Dorothy Cotton, daughter of Simon Bradstreet, Rev. Seaborn Cotton was connected with the Bradstreet, Dudley, and Winthrop families. On the records both of Hampton and of Boston Mr. Pierce's name is written Pearce, but in the imprints of his publications it is printed Pierce.

At the time of her marriage Sarah Cotton was only a little more than seventeen years of age, having been born July 2, 1663. In those early days the means of communication between Boston and Hampton were quite limited, and it does not appear probable that if Richard Pierce was printing in London in 1679, he could have crossed the ocean, become acquainted with Sarah Cotton, prosecuted his suit, and married her on August 27, 1680. It would seem to be more in accordance with the natural course of events that the marriage of Richard Pierce and Sarah Cotton was the result of an attachment formed perhaps while he was attending school in Hampton, possibly under her father as a teacher, or while she was on a long visit to her relatives in Boston.

If Richard Pierce had been the proprietor of a printing office in London, he would have made some attempt to open one in Boston soon after his arrival; but there is no record of any such attempt. It would seem to be more reasonable to believe that Richard Pierce belonged to the Pierce family of Essex County, who came to Boston and served his apprenticeship with that master of his art, John Foster, under whose instruction he learned the secrets of the craft, and when the opportunity offered by the resignation of Sewall, imported a new press and types, and published books remarkable for excellent printing.

When Sewall's petition to be released from the management of the press had been granted, it is very probable that the restriction which allowed only one press to be operated in Boston was also removed, and the licensers were willing to grant permission to print to any respectable printer who might apply. This was Pierce's opportunity. After the death of Foster, presumably he had been employed by Samuel Green, Jr., but now, indorsed by the Dudley, Cotton, and Bradstreet families, he probably experienced no difficulty in obtaining a license to print, and opened an office on the present Washington Street, nearly opposite Avery Street, which he had fitted up with the latest improvements. He soon printed a book entitled, *The Doctrine of Divine Providence opened and applyed. By Increase Mather,* the imprint of which reads: *Boston in New England printed by Richard Pierce for Joseph Brunning, and are to be sold at his Shop at the Corner of Prison-Lane next the Exchange, 1684.*

As "To the Reader" is dated "Boston, N. E. Octobre 25, 1684," presumably the *Monumental Memorial,* the first of Mr. Steere's books, was printed after *The Doctrine of Divine Providence.* Mr. Steere did not arrive in Boston before October.

Although his ship left England the latter part of July, she encountered several gales which prolonged the passage, and did not arrive in Boston Harbor until the latter part of October. On October 24 and 27 several of the townsmen of Boston became surety to the town for eight families which arrived in the ship with Steere. One of the bonds dated October 24, 1684, states that William Obbison became surety for Thomas Wallis, blacksmith, and his family. He was the father of the seaborn child, which was born when the ship was off Newfoundland. It is probable that Richard Steere wrote the poem while on the ship, and as he would not wish to make a long stop in Boston, made arrangements for printing soon after his arrival.

During the next six years Pierce was very active printing nearly as many books as Green, thirty-five titles being known. He printed largely for the booksellers, more especially Joseph Brunning. On December 20, 1686, Sir Edmund Andros arrived in Boston with a commission from King James for the government of New England. According to his letter of instructions he was " to allow no printing press." Three weeks before his arrival Edward Randolph, Secretary, who had been appointed licenser of the press by Andros, sent to Samuel Green, Jr., the following order:

" Mr. Green

I am commanded by Mr. Secretary Randolph to give you notice that you do not proceed to print any Almanack without having his approbation for the same.

Yours
Benj. Bullivant."

John Dunton, the London bookseller, who visited Boston in 1686, speaks very pleasantly of Dr. Bullivant. He says:

" From Dr. Oakes I pass to my good friend Dr. Bullivant, formerly my fellow citizen in London: I must consider him both as a gentleman and as a physician. As a gentleman he came of a noble family, but his good qualities exceeded his birth. He is a great master of the English tongue, and the Northampton people find him a universal scholar: his knowledge of the laws fitted him for the office of attorney-general which was conferred upon him on the revolution in Boston."

It does not appear that the command of Randolph had any effect, as the almanac for 1687 appeared with Green's name as usual. On the public documents, however, the imprint reads, " Boston. Printed by Richard Pierce, printer to the Honorable His Majesty's President & Council of this His Majesties Territory and Dominions of New England," which shows that Pierce had displaced Green as Colonial printer.

In the autumn of 1689 Samuel Green, Jr., printed at Boston *The Present State of the New English Affairs*, a single sheet, folio, printed on one side only, which contained an interesting letter from Rev. Increase Mather, then in England, and matters of importance relating to New England. A single copy only is in existence, and whether or not at other times Green printed similar sheets is unknown, but it is hard to believe that he made only one venture. On September 25, 1690, Richard Pierce printed for Benjamin Harris a similar publication, containing three printed pages, entitled *Publick Occurrences. Both Foreign and Domestic*, which has been alluded to frequently as the first newspaper printed in the English colonies. In the text accompanying a fac-simile reprint of *The Present State of the New English Affairs*, published by our worthy secretary, William Green Shillaber, he argues that Pierce or Harris copied Green's idea, and makes a seemingly just claim that the honor of printing the first newspaper in the English colonies belongs to Samuel Green, Jr.

The imprint of *An Almanac . . . for the Christian Year 1691. By Henry Newman* reads, *Printed by R. Pierce for Benjamin Harris at the London Coffee House in Boston, 1691.* As the almanac begins with January it must have been printed in 1690. It is almost certain that as a printer Richard Pierce was connected with the best-known book of the Colonial press, for the almanac of which the title has just been quoted advertises on its last leaf, " There is now in the Press, and will suddenly be extant a Second Impression of the New England Primer enlarged." It is not probable that Pierce would advertise the publications of any other printer in the books he was printing, and it is therefore reasonable to suppose that the imprint of the first edition of the *New England Primer* read, *Printed by R. Pierce for Benjamin Harris at the London Coffee House in Boston, 1690.*

Only one other book having the imprint of Richard Pierce in 1691 has been found. It is *A Scriptural Catechism. . . . By Cotton Mather*, the imprint of which reads, *Boston printed by R. Pierce for Nicholas Buttolph, at the corner Shop, next to Gutteridges Coffee House 1691*, which corresponds to where the Ames Building now stands.

His wife died in August, 1690, and Sewall records in his *Diary*, " Monday Aug. 4, 1690. Mrs. Pierce buried near the Tomb of her Grandfather Cotton." Whether Richard Pierce was a victim of the small-pox is not known, but he is supposed to have died in 1691, as his name is no longer found in the imprints, and his press shortly after passes into the possession of Benjamin Harris.

Bartholomew Green

Bartholomew Green

BARTHOLOMEW GREEN, the son of Samuel Green, was born at Cambridge, October 12, 1666. He served his apprenticeship with his father, by whom he was taught the art of printing. In 1687, when he was twenty-one years of age, he is found living in Boston, where there was a much better prospect for business than in Cambridge. Presumably he was employed by his brother Samuel Green, Jr., although at that time Richard Pierce was doing a large printing business in Boston. He was successful in his business affairs, and in 1690 married Mary Short, daughter of Clement Short, of Kittery, who was born about 1666. After the death of his brother in July, 1690, he managed his brother's business until September 16 of the same year, when in a disastrous fire the building containing his brother's printing office was nearly destroyed. Taking with him such portion of his brother's printing materials as he had been able to save from the fire, he returned to Cambridge and was admitted as a partner into the business of his father, the imprints of the books published by the new firm reading, *Cambridge. Printed by S. G. & B. G.* One of the books printed by the new firm was Rev. John Cotton's *Spiritual Milk for Babes*, translated into the Indian language by Rev. Grindal Rawson, the imprint of which reads, *Cambridge: Printenop nashpe Samuel Green kah Bartholomew Green.* With their old and battered presses they could not compete successfully with the Boston office, and it is probable that Samuel Green, being about eighty years old, and beginning to feel the infirmities of age, did not feel quite equal to the struggle and con-

cluded to retire from business. The partnership therefore was
dissolved early in 1692, and there was no more printing in Cambridge for nearly one hundred years.

Bartholomew Green went to Boston, and during 1692 printed
several books, some of which were *Printed by Bartholomew Green*
and others by *Bartholomew Green and John Allen*. The only
press in Boston at this time was the press which had belonged
to Richard Pierce, who is supposed to have died early in 1691.
After Pierce ceased to print, all the books printed in Boston in
1691 bore in their imprints the names of *Benjamin Harris and
John Allen*. During 1692 the imprints read, *Printed by Benjamin
Harris, by Benjamin Harris and John Allen, by Bartholomew Green,
by Bartholomew Green and John Allen,* and *by John Allen.* It is
very probable that the press remained in the possession of the
executors of the estate of Richard Pierce, and was hired by the
above-named printers as occasion demanded, and operated either
jointly or separately, as the printing jobs were taken.

Early in 1693 the press apparently comes into the possession of
Benjamin Harris, and during the first six months of that year he
appears to have been the only printer in Boston, and his name
alone is found in the imprints. The buying of the press, however, did not suppress Green. He secured another press and
applied for a license to print, which was granted, as appears by
the following record taken from the *Minutes of the General Assembly of Massachusetts*:

" June 6, 1693. Bartholomew Green, printer, is allowed to
set up his press and exercise his trade within the Town of Boston for the printing of what shall be duly licensed and nothing
else."

Mr. Green set up his press in a small wooden building on
Washington Street about twenty-five feet south of Avon Street.
Whether his press was a new one, or one of the College presses,
is not known, but as he was to compete with a comparatively

THE
SPIRIT
OF
MAN:

O R,

Some Meditations (by way of *Essay*) on
the Sense of that Scripture.

1 Thef. 5. 23. *And the very God of Peace Sancti-
fie you wholly, and I pray God, your whole Spirit,
and Soul, and Body, be Preserved Blameless unto the Coming of our Lord Jesus Christ.*

By *Charles Morton*, Minister of the Gospel
at *Charlstown* in *New-England*.

Mal. 3. 16. *Take heed to your Spirit.*
Luke 19. 55. *Ye know not what manner
of* Spirit *you are of.*

Boston *Printed by* B. Harris, *for* Duncan
Campbell, *at the* Dock-Head, *over-a-
gainst the* Conduit. 1693.

new press, controlled by that enterprising publisher Benjamin Harris, it is not probable that he would handicap himself with a second-hand press of an antiquated pattern. He used on his press the new types which his brother had bought a few years previously.

Apparently the first book printed by Green in his own shop was:

Acts and Laws, Passed by the Great and General Court or Assembly of their Majesties Province of the Massachusetts Bay in New England. Convened and held at Boston the Thirty-first Day of May 1693. Printed by Bartholomew Green, and Sold by Samuel Phillips, 1693.

The *Acts* passed at the previous Session, or Fourth Session of the first General Court held under the Provincial Charter of 1692, which " begun at Boston the Eighth Day of June, 1692, and Continued by several Adjournments unto Thursday the Second of March following," was *Printed by Benjamin Harris, Printer to His Excellency the Governour and Council, 1693,"* by which it appears that Benjamin Harris had been superseded as government printer by Bartholomew Green. Until August, 1695, all the books printed by Green bore his name alone in the imprint, and the *Acts and Laws Passed by the Great and General Court . . . . Begun . . . the Twenty-ninth of May 1695,* was *Printed by Bartholomew Green, Printer to the Governour and Council. 1695,* but the *Acts and Laws. . . . Begun . . . the Twenty-ninth of May, 1695, and continued by Adjournment until Wednesday the Fourteenth of August following* was *Printed by Bartholomew Green and John Allen, Printers to the Governour and Council. 1695.*

Late in 1694, or early in 1695, Benjamin Harris had returned to London, leaving his relative Vavasour Harris to close up his business affairs. Evidently John Allen superintended his printing contracts, as the imprints of the books from the Harris press during 1695 read, *Printed by John Allen, for Vavasour Harris,* or

Printed by John Allen, and Vavasour Harris. After the printing contracts had been completed the Harris press was for sale, and probably John Allen could have it if he so desired. He had influential friends, and if he opened a printing office might possibly secure the government printing. Green evidently saw that it would be better to combine rather than to compete, and therefore formed a partnership with Allen, which brought both offices under one management. What were the terms of the partnership is not known, but it continued until 1704. In 1704 the partnership between Green and Allen is apparently dissolved. Allen retires, but Green continues the business, and from this time until his death the name of Bartholomew Green alone appears in the imprint. On October 14, 1705, Bartholomew Green bought the land on which stood the building which he had occupied as a printing office.

April 24, 1704, Bartholomew Green printed for John Campbell the first number of the first continuous newspaper printed in the British colonies of North America, namely, *The Boston News Letter.* With the exception of from November, 1707, to October, 1711, this newspaper was printed by Green and his successors until 1776.

While serving his apprenticeship with his father in Cambridge, Bartholomew Green had been employed in printing the second edition of the Indian Bible, and had learned to print books in the Indian Language, which was of great service to him later.

In 1699, with John Allen, he printed *A Confession of Faith owned and consented unto by the Elders and Messengers of the Churches assembled at Boston in New England, May 12, 1680.* It was first published in Boston by John Foster in 1680. Having been translated into the Indian language by Rev. Grindal Rawson, it was now printed with English and Indian on opposite pages, by Green and Allen.

In 1705 Green printed with English and Indian in alternate

Ebenezer Pemberton

The Order of the
Gofpel,

Profeffed and Practifed by the
Churches of CHRIST in
New-England, Juftified, by the
Scripture, and by the Writings
of many Learned men, both
Ancient and Modern Divines ;
In Anfwer to feveral Queftions
relating to Church Difcipline

By *Increafe Mather*, Prefident of
Harvard Colledge in *Cambridge*, and
Teacher of a Church at *Bofton*
in *New England*.

Jer. 2. 21, 36 *I had planted thee a noble
vine, wholly a right feed---why gaddeft thou
about fo much to change thy way?---*
Col 2. 5. *Joying and beholding* your Order,
--- and the Steadfaftnefs *of your Faith*.

BOSTON, Printed by B. *Green*, & *J. Allen*,
for *Benjamin Eliot*, at his Shop under the
Weft End of the Town-Houfe, 1700

A

DISCOURSE

Concerning the

Wonderfulnels

OF

CHRIST.

Delivered in
Several SERMONS.

By Nehemiah Walter, M. A.
Paſtor of the Church in *Roxbury.*

Phil. iii. 8.
*I count all things but loſs, for the excellency of
the knowledge of Chriſt Jeſus.*

Boſton in New-England :
Printed by *B. Green,* for *Eleazer Philips,*
at his Shop at the lower end of King Street.
1 7 1 3.

paragraphs *The Hatchets, to hew down the Tree of Sin which bears the Fruit of Death. Or, the Laws, by which the Magistrates are to punish Offences, among the Indians, as well as among the English* supposed to have been written by Cotton Mather.

In 1706 he printed with Indian and English on opposite pages, *An Epistle to the Christian Indians. By Cotton Mather.*

In 1709 he printed *The Massachuset Psalter or Psalms of David*, etc., with Indian and English on the same page, in columns separated by a rule. The translation was made by Experience Mayhew. "Next to the Indian Bible this book is considered the most important monument of the Massachuset language." In printing this book Green was assisted by James Printer, an Indian who had been taught the art of printing by Samuel Green, Bartholomew's father. A copy of this book at the sale of the Brinley Library in 1878 brought one hundred and thirty-five dollars.

Green printed in 1720 an *Indian Primer or First Book by which Children may know truly to read the Indian language. And Milk for Babes.* It is a small duodecimo of one hundred and sixty-eight pages, and brought in the Brinley sale one hundred and ten dollars.

Besides books in the Indian language Green printed two very interesting and exceedingly scarce books relating to the Indian wars, both of which have been many times reprinted.

The first contains the story of the captivity of the Reverend John Williams. The title reads :

The Redeemed Captive, Returning to Zion. A Faithful History of Remarkable Occurrences in the Captivity and Deliverance of Mr. John Williams, Minister of the Gospel in Deerfield, who, in the Desolation which befel that Plantation, by an Incursion of the French & Indians, was by them carried away, with his Family, unto Canada, (With) A Sermon preached by him, upon his Return, at Boston, Dec. 5, 1706. Boston, Printed by B. Green, 1707.

It is a small duodecimo and contains one hundred and ten pages.

The second relates to the Indian wars, and is one of the rarest books of its class. The writer once bid at an auction sale five hundred dollars for a copy, but did not secure it. After the sale he was informed by his successful competitor that if he had made one more bid he would have obtained it. The title reads:

Entertaining Passages relating to Philip's War which began in the Month of June, 1675. As also of Expeditions more lately made against the Common Enemy, and Indian Rebels, in the Eastern Parts of New-England. With some Account of the Divine Providence towards Benj. Church Esqr. By T. C. Boston: Printed by B. Green, in the Year 1716.

It is a small quarto, and contains one hundred and twenty-four pages.

Mr. Green was so successful in his business that he was obliged to enlarge his printing office, which he did by building in the rear until it was twice its original size, and was thus enabled to house another press.

His wife, Mary Short, died March 26, 1709, and he married for second wife Jane, daughter of Jacob and Hannah (Sewall) Tappan, niece of Judge Sewall, born September 28, 1674. By his first wife he had ten children, and by his second wife two. On April 17, 1719, he was elected deacon of the Old South Church, which office he held at his death. He died December 28, 1732. The following notice of his death is extracted from *The Boston News-Letter* of January 4, 1733:

" Bartholomew Green was a person generally known and esteemed among us, as a very humble and exemplary Christian, one who had much of that primitive Christianity in him which has always been the distinguishing glory of New England. We may further remember his eminency for a strict observing the

The High Attainment.

A Brief DISCOURSE

Concerning

Resignation

to the WILL of GOD;

A Glorious DUTY incumbent on
every CHRISTIAN,

AND

Containing in it, the very *Spirit*,
and Comfort, and Glory of

CHRISTIANITY.

Omnem Diem inter amissos deputate,
in quo, Dei Amore, propriam non
fregistis voluntatem.

Taulerus.

BOSTON : Printed by *B. Green,*
& *J. Allen,* for *Nicholas Boone,* at his
Shop near the Old-Meeting-House,
1 7 0 3.

sabbath; his household piety; his keeping close and diligent to the work of his calling; his meek and peaceful spirit; his caution of publishing anything offensive, light or hurtful; and his tender sympathy to the poor and afflicted. He always spoke of the wonderful spirit of piety that prevailed in the land in his youth with a singular pleasure."

From Drake's *History of Boston* we extract the following:

"On the 30th of Jan. 1734 the Printing House belonging to the widow and children of the late Deacon Green at the South End was burned. In it two printing-presses were destroyed; also a great quantity of type: very little was saved. The fire took about 12 o'clock at night. No other buildings burned."

John Allen

John Allen

THE imprint of *The Daniel Catcher* reads, *Printed in the year 1713.* Neither Rev. Thomas Prince nor that eminent bibliographer James Hammond Trumbull, LL.D., ever discovered the name of the printer or the town in which it was printed, although Dr. Trumbull says doubtingly that it was printed by Timothy Green at New London. After searching the various bibliographies and receiving no help, it was found that the only way in which the question could be solved was by comparing the publications of the contemporary printers with this book. Without wearying our readers with further explanations the simple statement is made, that a careful comparison and a critical examination of a large number of books printed by all the printers in New York, New London, and Boston, convinced the writer that John Allen was the printer, and Boston the town in which it was printed. The types used in printing this book are the same as those used by Allen in other books printed by him, and are not found in the books printed by any other printer, and the conclusion that John Allen of Boston was the printer was irresistible.

This conclusion was arrived at in October, 1904; the above paragraph was written at that time, and read to the Club at the monthly meeting in January, 1905. In October, 1905, Dr. Samuel A. Green, LL.D., directed the attention of the writer to an advertisement which he had seen while on a visit to the library of the American Antiquarian Society, at Worcester, Mass., in a number of *The Boston News Letter*, which proves that the conclusion was correct, as John Allen was printer for

Nicholas Boon. Our associate, Mr. Nathaniel Paine, has very kindly furnished the photographic fac-simile of this advertisement.

John Allen was the nephew of the Rev. James Allen of England, one of the ejected ministers who arrived in Boston in 1662, and became pastor of the First Church. He was born in England about 1660. Whether or not he was related to John Allen, who printed in 1669 *The Mystery of Israel's Salvation. By Increase Mather*, does not appear. He was apprenticed to and taught the art of printing by George Larkin "printer at the Two Swans, without Bishopsgate, London." In 1686 he decided to join his uncle in America.

In a letter to his wife dated October 25, 1685, John Dunton gives his reasons for making a visit to New England, in which he says, " And I must confess 'twas the Hopes of Gold (with a little pleasure into the bargain) that has now engaged ten merry boys of us to plow the ocean and like souldiers of fortune to run all hazards that we might obtain our end." The " ten merry boys" were Messrs. Stevens, Bolt, Roswell, Charles Martin, Jr., Weaver, Pain, Hasswell, Herrick, Allen, a printer, his assistant Mr. Palmer, and himself. They left Gravesend on October 16, about three in the afternoon, in the ship " Susan and Thomas" belonging to Boston, Mass., of which the master was Thomas Jenner. She was of 150 tons' burden, manned by sixteen sailors, and carried about thirty passengers, many of whom were fleeing for safety after the defeat of Monmouth at Sedgemore. The passage was long and stormy, and the ship did not arrive at Boston until about February 10, 1686.

Dunton gives a humorous description of a storm at sea which was so dreadful that " even the sailors who seldom pray, came to the passengers desiring us that for God's sake we would all go to prayers," fearing that the ship would not hold out for an hour. " The seamen's desiring us to go to prayer put

The Boston News-Letter.

Numb. 484.

Published by Authority.

From Monday August 17. to Monday August 24. 1713.

Hamburgh, May 9. N. S. 1713.

WE have received Advice, that the Treaty for the Surrender of Tonningen being broke off, by reason that the King of Denmark insisted to be sole Master of it as soon as should be evacuated by the Swedes, with out admitting any of the Troops of Hol-

States have frequent Conferences with their Deputies about settling the number of the Troops they are to keep in Pay in time of Peace; but they have not yet fixed the same, and will defer it till the Execution of the Treaties concluded with France. Upon the earnest Instances of the Ministers of Holstein, the Deputies of the States had yesterday a Conference with the Ministers of the Czar and King Augustus, wherein they exhorted them to a reasonable Accommodation with Count Steinbock, and re-

(1)

Advertisements.

A Cast Hammer, Anvil Plates, and all other needful Cast Iron work for a Forge, or Iron works, all New, to be Sold by *Nathanael Thomas,* Esqr. at *Marshfield.*

A Large Brick Dwelling House, Stable, Out Houses, Gardens, and a considerable Tract of Land adjoining, fronting to two Streets, *viz.* Salem & Charter Street, in the North End of *Boston,* either to be Lett or Sold; Inquire of *Spencer Phipps* of *Cambridge* Esq. or *Eliakem Hutchinson* of *Boston* Esq. and know further.

JUst Published, *The Daniel Catcher*: The Life of the Prophet Daniel; in a POEM: To which is added, *Lovi's Felicities, Heaven's Allowances,* a Blank Poem, with several other Poems. By R. S. Sold by *Nicholas Boone* at the Sign of the Bible in *Cornhill.*

(2)

me in mind of that saying, 'He that would learn to pray, let him go to sea,' at which several of us did. But even in the confusion we had some angry words, for upon the Seamen desiring us to go to Prayers, one of our passengers pulled out 'The Crumbs of Comfort' [a prayer book] which displeased some of the rest. . . . But though some in our ship wanted such helps as these yet there were others that did not, and particularly Mr. Charles Martin and Mr. Allen, who not only prayed with us extempore, but sung a Psalm, which seemed like that at Tyburn, sung by condemned criminals before their execution. I know not how 't was with my fellow passengers, but for myself I was too sad to sing."

Dunton says that Mr. Allen the printer was going to his uncle, who had invited him over, and from whom he expected preferment. In a letter to George Larkin, dated Boston, March 25, 1686, Dunton says, "and I think myself obliged to send this part of my rambles to you, my dear friend, both as your letter to Mr. John Allen, your quondam servant (and my fellow traveller hither) speaks so kindly of me and engages me to this talk: as also as a testimony of the respect I have for you, for your so boldly appearing for the true English liberties and Protestant religion even at a time when it could not be done without danger. . . . I rambled with John Allen to dine with his Reverend uncle of that name. He is a grave ancient divine and now pastor of the new church in Boston. All that I shall say of him more is that he is very humble and very rich and can be generous if he pleases." Rev. James Allen resided in a stone mansion on the corner of the present Beacon and Somerset streets, lately occupied by the Congregational House. John Dunton secured lodgings with Richard Wilkins, the bookseller, whose house and shop were on the site of the present Sears Building, while John Allen engaged rooms in what had been, a short time previous, the famous Ship Tavern, on the north side of Williams Court, but which now was let for offices and lodgings.

It is very probable that John Allen secured employment as a printer, for in this same letter to Larkin, Dunton, after describing the booksellers of Boston, proceeds to tell about the printers, and after noticing Samuel Green, Jr., says, "and here likewise was Mr. John Allen, your quondam servant, who was so well known to you, that I need say the less of him; But yet being both my Friend and Fellow-Traveller, that for four Months together run the same risque of Fortune with me, I cannot but say something of him: His Aspect has something so extraordinary in it, that whoever does but look upon him, will make no Scruple to give him the Title of My Lord: He is Master of an Excellent Mediocrity of Temper, for if Fortune smile, it never elates him; neither is he cast down if she Frowns. And under some more than ordinary Disappointment, I have known him to drown his Sorrows in a glass of Cyder; Fortune has plaid him some slippery Tricks so that he'll never Trust her: and if anything falls out, better than he expects, tis welcome."

The first book that has been found with which Allen's name is connected is *A Sermon Preached at Roxbury on a Fast Day July 26, 1687. By James Allen, Teacher to the First Gathered Church in Boston. Boston: Printed for Job How and John Allen and are to be sold at Mr. Samuel Greens by the South Meeting House 1687.*

Job and John How were brothers who had worked in the printing office of George Larkin, one of whom married Larkin's daughter. They visited Boston in 1686, but remained only a few months. It is probable that the Hows and Allen, fellow craftsmen, found employment with Samuel Green, Jr., and were the actual printers of the above-mentioned sermon, although using Green's press. From 1686 to 1690 Allen is supposed to have been employed by Green, but upon the latter's death in

Seasonable
𝕸𝖊𝖉𝖎𝖙𝖆𝖙𝖎𝖔𝖓𝖘
BOTH FOR
WINTER & SUMMER.
Being the Substance of Two
SERMONS.

By **J. Mather**, D. D.

Psal. 71. 17, 18. *O God, thou hast taught me from my youth : and hitherto have I declared thy wondrous works. Now also when I am old and gray-headed, O God, forsake me not : until I have shewed thy strength unto this Generation, and thy power to every one that is to come.*

Prov. 15. 23. *A word spoken in due season, how good is it ?*

Boston, Printed by *John Allen*, 1712.

1690, and a few months later the destruction of his office by fire, is supposed to have associated himself with Richard Pierce. In 1691 he had a business arrangement with Benjamin Harris, by which both of their names appeared in the imprints of the books printed that year. In 1692 he prints sometimes alone, sometimes with Harris, and occasionally with Bartholomew Green. In 1693 Harris is supposed to have bought the Pierce press, and presumably Allen was employed by Harris during 1693 and 1694. In 1695 he assists Vavasour Harris in closing up Benjamin Harris's business, and in the imprints of the books from the Harris press his name is joined with Vavasour Harris. From 1696 to 1704 he was in partnership with Bartholomew Green, the only two presses in the colony — namely, Bartholomew Green's and Benjamin Harris's being now under the control of the firm, and the imprints of the books read, *Printed by Bartholomew Green and John Allen.*

In 1704 the partnership between Green and Allen apparently is dissolved, and Allen's name no longer appears in the imprints.

It is supposed Allen may have made a visit to England at this time, as nothing is heard of him until 1707, when he opened a printing office in Pudding Lane, now Devonshire Street, where he carried on the business in his own name. In November he began to print *The Boston News Letter* for the proprietor, Mr. John Campbell, in an early number of which he published the following advertisement, viz. : " These are to give notice that there lately came from London a Printing Press, with all sorts of good new Letter, which is now set up in Pudding Lane near the Post-Office in Boston for publick use : Where all persons that have anything to print may be served on reasonable terms."

Here he continued to print books as well as the newspaper, until his establishment was destroyed in the great fire which broke out October 2, 1711. When a new building had been erected on the old site, he fitted up a new printing office, and continued the business until 1727, about which time he died, although the record of his death has not been found.

It is very probable that the second impression of *The New England Primer* was printed under his supervision, and that the success of that book turned his attention to printing school books. In 1702 he printed with Bartholomew Green the first American edition of *Sententiae Pueriles, Anglo-Latinae or Sentences for Children, English and Latin*, a boy's text-book which had long been popular in England, and of which many editions were published in Boston. He also published *The Young Secretary's Guide. By Thomas Hill.* The earliest copy printed in New England that has been found is *The Third Edition. Boston in New England. Printed by B. Green & J. Allen for S. Phillips at the Brick-Shop, 1703.* The twenty-seventh English edition was published in 1764; the twenty-fourth American edition, in 1750. In a copy of the sixth American edition, the imprint of which reads, *Boston. Reprinted for Nicholas Boone at the Bible in Cornhill. 1727*, is an introductory preface entitled *The Printer to the Reader*, signed by J. A. (John Allen). He says "that a more useful book on this subject never came to my hands. It has sufficiently recommended itself to the world already by the sale of five large impressions, all of which were sold in a short time." As the various editions were printed for and sold by different booksellers, and apparently printed by Allen, it would seem that Allen was considered to hold a sort of copyright on this book, which was respected by the other printers. In 1730 the seventh edition was printed by Thomas Fleet, which leads to the belief that Allen had died, and his office had passed to Fleet.

Timothy Green

Charity Sorn

Timothy Green

AS a brief biography of Timothy Green has been printed in *Early Boston Booksellers*, it has been thought advisable not to repeat it here. The opportunity is taken, however, to correct an error which appeared in that sketch, and to add some other facts.

We have been informed by our associate, Mr. William Green Shillaber, that in his genealogical researches concerning the Green family he has found proof that Timothy Green was a *brother* and not a *son* of Samuel Green, Jr., the Boston printer. He was a son of Samuel Green, the Cambridge printer, by his second wife, Sarah, daughter of Elder Jonas Clark, and was born at Cambridge in 1679. His father died January 1, 1701–2, and on August 2, 1707, the widow sold the homestead, and to the deed of sale these sons affixed their names, namely, Jonas Green of New London, mariner, Bartholomew Green, printer, Joseph Green, tailor, Timothy Green, printer, — all of Boston. Corroboration is found in a letter to Governor Talcott, dated February 12, 1732–3, written by Timothy Green shortly after the death of Bartholomew Green in Boston, in which he writes of a visit " to my (then sick but now dead) brother."

Undoubtedly Timothy served his apprenticeship with his brother Bartholomew, but when arrived at the age of twenty-one he opened a printing office on his own account, in Boston, the imprint of his first book bearing the date 1700. He was successful, and in 1708 was invited by the Governor and Council of the Connecticut Colony to remove to the Colony and become the Colonial printer. He did not accept the invitation, but declined in favor of Thomas Short, the brother-in-law of Bartholomew Green. Short accepted the appointment, removed to New London, set up a press there, and became the first printer of Connecticut. Where he obtained his press does not appear, but it was not an expensive one, as in the inventory of his estate taken in 1712 the printing plant was appraised at £45. In 1709 he printed several broadsides, the proclamation for a fast on June 15, 1709, being apparently the first issue of the new printing office. During the same year he printed the Session Laws from October, 1702, to October, 1708 inclusive, making a folio volume of twenty-four pages. It had no title-page, the signatures were marked Hh–Nn, and the pages were numbered 119 to 142. It was evidently intended to complete the volume entitled *Acts and Laws Of His Majesties Colony of Connecticut in New-England. Boston. Printed by Bartholomew Green and John Allen. 1702*, as that volume ended with signature Gg and page 118. Apparently the twenty-four pages printed by Thomas Short represent the first book printed in Connecticut.

In 1710 Short printed the well-known Saybrook Confession of Faith, a small octavo of one hundred and sixteen pages, which has the reputation of being the first complete book printed in Connecticut. Mr. William Green Shillaber, who has in his possession a remarkably fine copy of this excessively scarce book, has kindly furnished the following title-page:

A | Confession | of | Faith | Owned and Consented to by the | Elders and Messengers | Of the Churches | In the Colony of Connecticut in | New-England, | Assembled by Delegation at Say-Brook | September 9th, 1708. | Eph. 4. 5. One Faith, | Col. 2. 5. Joying and beholding your | Order and the steadfastness of your | Faith in Christ. | New-London in N. E. | Printed by Thomas Short, | 1710.

The contract which the General Assembly of the Connecticut Colony made in October, 1708, with Thomas Short reads as follows:

" Whereas Mr. Thomas Short of Boston, printer, hath now offered to this Court to print all the publick acts of this Colony (and the election sermon if desired,) every year, for four years, to commence at the first of May next ensuing, and to give a copie for every town or place in the Colony that hath a clerk or register, for the sum of fifty pounds a year in money, or other pay equivalent as stated in the country rate, and to find paper for the same; and also to find paper and print all orders for fasts and thanksgivings, and proclamations whatsoever, and give a copy for every society in the Colony, — and always to print the acts of the General Court within one month after the receipt of the copie of them, (if not above eight sheets,) and all other pub- lick business immediately upon his receipt of the copy, and to send the printed copies with all convenient speed after they are printed to the several county sheriffs, to be by them conveyed to the towns, places and societys for whom they are, — and also to print our laws which are now in manuscript for twenty shillings a sheet (and find paper for the same,) in like pay as aforesaid, and to give a copy for every town or place as aforesaid, well folded, sticht and covered with painted paper: — upon consideration whereof,

" It is now ordered, enacted and concluded by this Court, That there shall be paid to the said Mr. Thomas Short out of the publick treasury of this Colony by the Treasurer, the sum and sums expressed in his above proposals, for the time therein speci- fied; provided he shall set up a printing press in this Colony, and perform the conditions on his part in the said proposalls expressed." [1]

Thomas Short died September 27, 1712, and the Acts and Laws passed at the October session of the General Assembly, and probably all other " public business " until the expiration of his contract, May 1, 1713, was printed by Bartholomew Green at Boston.

[1] Connecticut Colonial Records, V, 69.

The invitation to become the Colonial printer was again extended to Timothy Green, which he accepted, and pursuant to a vote of the General Assembly passed at the May session, 1713, went to New London and took over the printing office of Thomas Short.   His contract with the General Assembly was practically the same as that made with Short, and his term of service, which presumably began on May 1, 1713, was for four years.   In a petition to the General Assembly, regarding his salary, dated October 22, 1745, Green says:

" In 1713 I came up and a Council was called at New London who agreed with me to give me fifty pounds per annum to print all the laws in their Several Sessions they shall hold yearly, all the proclamations and if the Colony See Cause the Election Sermon, and find paper.   Accordingly I have done so every year since 1713."

Although Timothy Green became *Printer to his Honour the Governour and Council [of Connecticut]* in 1713, yet he did not give up his Boston office, for in 1714 he printed in Boston for the Rev. Samuel Moodey a book entitled *Judas the Traitor hung up in Chains*, etc.   Presumably he travelled from office to office as occasion required.   By the terms of his contract Green was bound " to print the acts of the General Court within one month after the receipt of the copy of them (if not above eight sheets) " and probably the first issue of his press in Connecticut was *Acts and Laws, Passed by the General Court or Assembly Of Her Majesty's Colony of Connecticut in New England.   Begun and Held at Hartford upon Thursday the Fourteenth Day of May; .... 1713. And continued by several Adjournments to the Twenty Ninth Day of the Same Month.   Printed at New-London, by T. Green, by Order of his Honour the Governour, and Council.   1713.*   It is a folio of four pages, and the edition was three hundred copies.

Green, however, was also bound by his contract " to print the

The Doleful STATE of the

Damned ;

Especially such as go to

HELL

From under the

GOSPEL;

Aggravated from their Apprehensions of the SAINTS Happiness in

HEAVEN

Being the Substance of several SERMONS, Preached at *York*, in the Province of *Main-*

By Samuel Moodey, M. A.
Pastor of the Church of CHRIST there.

I. Thess. ii. 16 *Wrath is come upon them to the* UTTERMOST.

BOSTON: Printed & Sold by *Timothy Green* in Middle Street. Also Sold by *Benj. Eliot* in King Street. 1710.

Election Sermon if so desired," and it is possible that the election sermon for that year, the printed title-page of which reads, *The Necessity of Religion in Societies, etc. By Rev. John Bulkley. Election Sermon, May 14, 1713. Timothy Green. 1713,* a small octavo of seventy pages, may have been printed before the *Acts.*

August 10, 1714, Timothy Green with his family removed to New London, going by land and accompanied by several of his friends as far as Dedham. What became of his Boston press is unknown. It is possible it was bought by Thomas Fleet, the London printer, who on account of his religious opinions had been obliged to leave England secretly, and arrived at Boston a short time previous to Green's departure, where he opened a printing office. It is not probable that under such circumstances he could have brought a press with him from England.

January 28, 1702. Timothy Green and Mary Flint were married in Boston by Rev. Cotton Mather.

He died at New London, aged seventy-eight, leaving six sons and one daughter. His eldest son, Timothy Green, Jr., born December 6, 1703, after having been instructed in the art of printing by his father, removed to Boston, where, having formed a partnership with Samuel Kneeland, he carried on a printing business for twenty-five years; but upon the death of his brother Samuel he closed his partnership with Kneeland, returned to New London, and entered into partnership with his father, who soon resigned the whole business to him.

Samuel Green, son of Timothy, was born April 22, 1706. He was taught printing by his father, and was taken into partnership with him. He died in May, 1752, leaving a family of nine children, three of them sons, who became printers.

Jonas, another son of Timothy, was born December 24, 1722, and was also instructed in the art of printing by his father. Thomas, in his *History of Printing in America*, says of him:

" The government of Maryland having offered a generous consideration to a printer who would establish a press in Annapolis, he closed with the proposal and in 1740 opened a printing house in that city. He was appointed printer for the Colony, and had granted to him an annual salary of £500 currency."

James Printer

Sacred Heart

James Printer

THERE was one other printer engaged in the printing of books who, although it is not known that he ever owned a press or opened an office on his own account, yet seems to demand that some notice should be taken of him. He was an Indian known as James Printer, or James the Printer. He was born at the Indian town called Hassanamesitt, now Grafton, in the county of Worcester, Massachusetts. His father was Naoas, one of the Indians converted by Rev. John Eliot and deacon of the church of Christian Indians in that town. James was instructed at the Indian charity school at Cambridge, and in 1659 was put apprentice to Samuel Green to learn the printer's business, with whom he remained until 1675, when he joined the Indians who were engaged in war with the English. He, however, took advantage of the " Declaration " put forth by the Council at Boston, signifying that such Indians as did, within fourteen days, come in to the English, might hope for mercy, and returned to Boston July 8, 1676. He was of great assistance to Green and Johnson in printing the first edition of the Indian Bible, 1661–1663. He was absolutely necessary to Samuel Green when printing the second edition of the Indian Bible, 1680–1685. In 1683, in writing to the Hon. Robert Boyle at London, Rev. John Eliot says: " I desire to see it done before I die, and I am so deep in years, that I cannot expect to live long; besides, we have but one man, viz. the Indian Printer, that is able to compose the sheets, and correct the press with understanding." He is supposed to have been employed by the Greens in printing all their Indian publications,

A Monumental Memorial,
etc.

FACSIMILE REPRODUCTION

By permission of the Massachusetts Historical Society

A

MONUMENTAL

MEMORIAL

OF

MARINE

MERCY

BEING

An Acknowledgment of an High Hand of
Divine Deliverance on the *Deep*
in the Time of diſtreſs,

IN

A Late Voyage from *Boſton* in *New-England*
To *LONDON*, Anno 1683.

In a Poem. By *Richard Steere*.

To which is added *Another* Occaſioned by Several
Remarkable Paſſages happening at the *Birth*
of a *Male Child* on Board the *ſame Ship*
in *her* Voyage *Returning* 1684.

By the ſame *Author* then a *Paſſenger*.

Printed at *BOSTON* in *New-England* by
Richard Pierce for *James Cowse* Stationer
Anno 1684.

To the Reader

Reader

I Here prefent thee with an Impartial Narrative, Collected from a Diurnall, and other Credible Informations of fome Perfons who had a fhare in this fo never to be forgotten a Deliverance, and at whofe Impertunity it was Reduced into this fmall Tract, and fhrouded in the modern Attire of Meafure and Cadency, whofe even and eafie Pace being more Alluring and Captivating (Efpecially with youth, or the Critticaly Ingenious of this Age) than the Elaborate Volumns of Profe left to us by our Worthy Anceftors, may probably the fooner Decoy or Invite thy Perufal .

I could not Conveniently avoyd the ufe of fome Sea phrafes The Subject being a Sea Deliverance, tho they may feem improper and unintelligible to a Land Capacity . And if I have erred in miffap-
plying

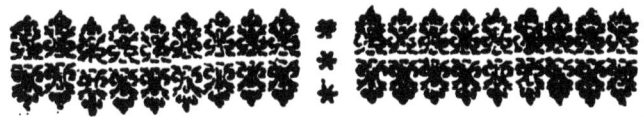

To the Reader

Reader

I Here *prefent thee with an Impartial Narrative,*
Collected from a Diurnall , *and other Credible*
Informations of fome Perfons who had a fhare
in this fo never to be forgotten *a Deliverance ,*
and at whofe Importunity it was Reduced into this
fmall Tract , *and fhrouded in the modern Attire of*
Meafure *and* Cadency, *whofe even and eafie Pace*
being more Alluring and Captivating (Efpecially
with youth, or the Crittically Ingenious of this Age)
than the Elaborate Volumns *of Profe left to us*
by our Worthy Anceftors , may probably the fooner
Decoy *or Invite thy Perufal .*

I could not Conveniently avoyd the ufe of fome
Sea phrafes *The Subject being a* Sea Deliverance ,
tho they may feem improper and unintelligible to a
Land Capacity . *And if I have erred in miffap-*
plying

To the Reader,

Mifapplying thofe Termes of Art, I hope the Ingenious Mariner will attribute it to the want of Experience in the Tarpolin *Tongue :*
  But to put a period to this Epiftle,

Read and Admire the Mercy, — *Tho' the Stile May make thee think it hardly worth the while.*

A

MONUMENTAL MEMORIAL

OF

MARINE MERCY &c.

Since Every *Quill* is silent to Relate
What being known must needs be wonder'd at
I take the boldness to present your *Eye*
With Safty's *Prospect* in Extremity,
Which tho not Cloath'd with *Academick* Skill,
Or lofty Raptures of a *Poet*'s Quill;
But wrapt in *raggs*, through which your eyes may see
The *Naked* Truth in plain simplicitee -
  I without further prologue *Lanch with* Ink
With Captain *Balston* in th' *Adventure Pinck*;
Who in *December* on the fourteenth day,
His Anchors *weigh'd* in *Massachusets* BAY,

New

New-England's Chiefest *Port,* and *fayling on,*
Soon *lay'd the Land* below the *Horizon* .

    The *Sea* was kind, the Sky ferene and clear,
All feem to fmile, no threating Frowns appear ;
Yet fometimes Clouds of Rain, of Hail, of Snow ,
Sometimes the *winds* more lofty, fometimes low ,

    The *Mariners* and *Paffengers a'board* ,
Enjoying what the Veffel did afford
With Satisfaction, and in full Content :
This good beginning was Encouragement
Of good fuccefs, in hope and expectation
The Ship might prove an *Ark* of prefervation ;
Her *fwelling fayls* gave her a nimble motion ,
Making her *Keel* to *plough* the Yeilding *Ocean,*
Whofe little *Billows* ftill her *Bow* out braves ,
Glideing Tryumphant o're the *Curled waves* .

    Thus for five weeks the gentler winds did play
Upon the *Oceans* Surface to convey
Our little *Pinck* , filling her plyant Sayles
With eafie *Breezes,* fweet *Topgallant Gailes* :
And now the *Mariners* by Judgment found   }
We did approach nigh to *Great Brittains* ground }
And therefore *heav'd* the *Deep-fea lead* to *found,* }
Which tho they *Fathom'd* not did Truth afford ,
For the fame night a *Land bird* came *a'board* ,
And the next morning we beheld two more
Which made the Judgment good they gave before

    Had we continu'd *thus* upon the Deep
We had bin Charm'd into a drowfie fleep
Of calme Security , nor had we known
The Excellence of *PRESERVATION;*

We had been Dumb and silent to Expreſs
Affeƈtedly the Voy'ges good ſucceſs .
  But to awake and Rowſe our ſleepy minds,
The *Po'wrs* above let looſe th' unruly winds ,
Heav'ns milder *Puffs* with violence at laſt
Let fly more fierce, and *blow* a ſtronger *Blaſt* :
The dark'ned Sky with gloomy *Clouds* o're ſpread,
Whoſe moiſt'ned *fleeces* have *Envcloped*
Tempeſtous Flaws which Iſſue more and more
In *Thunder's* Language, or as *Cannons* roar :
The weighty Seas Roul from the *Deeps* beneath .
Hill ſtands on *bill* by force of Heav'n blown breſth,
And from the *rocks foundatious* do ariſe
As tho reſolv'd to *ſtorm* th' *Impending* Skyes ;
Flaws from thoſe lofty *Battlements* are hurld ,
As to *a Chaos* they would ſhake the world :
Thus as between a warr of *Sea* and *Heaven,*
From place to place our little *Ship* is driven ;
And by the Seas toſt like a ball in ſport ,
From *wave to wave* in *Neptunes Tennis Court* .
  While thus the *winds* & *ſeas* their pow'rs diſpute
A neighb'ring objeƈt did our Eyes ſalute ,
A Sayle to windward ; (in Diſtreſs no doubt)
Who *Fir'd a Gun* and *heav'd* their *Colours out* ;
We *made* her *Engliſh,* but no help could give ,
The Lofty Seas found each enough to *live*
But in the morning we *to windward* were
And *Bearing down* reſolv'd to *ſpeak with her* ,
And underſtood ſhe from *Eaſt India* came,
Under Command of Captain *Hide* by Name
                               Byrden

Burden *six hundred Tuns* and *Ninety Men*
Having about ten *months* from *India* been,
And had bin *Beating* six *weeks* on the *Coast*
Wanting *Provis'on*, almost spent and Lost:
An Interval of *storms* became their freind,
And gave us leave some little help to lend:
The *storm* renewing its *Impetuous Force*
Did Each from Other further off Divorce,
Yet we might see them two or three dayes more,
But since have heard that they were drave *a, shore*
Somewhere in *Cornwall*, on the *Western Coast*,
And ev'ry Soul except two *Boyes* were lost.

   Still the resistless *winds* rebellious grow,
As they the *Universe* would Overthrow,
The pondrous *seas* like Rowling *Mountains* Rill,
Each *Billow* seeming an *Alpean* hill
By its prodigious Altitude: Despair
And fear of Danger, moves all lips to *pray'r*
Mixt with *Industry*, but *Industry* failes,
The *Pumps* are now in use but not the *Sayles*,
The Artist's *Quadrants* now are uselels grown,
For *Darkness* dwells upon our *Horizon*;
Thus we for sev'ral days upon the *Ocean*
Did *Ly a Hull*, keeping our *Pumps* in motion;
Till *January twenty sixth* at night,
A mighty *Sea* did *Overwhelm* us quite,
Which falling down with a resistless stroke
Both our Ships *Waste* (or well built *Gunwalls*) broke
And carr'd away: now seeming like a *Wreck*
From the *Fore castle* to the *Quarter Deck*,

                        The

The *Long boat*, *Windless*, *Capt stern*, with the blow
Besides two weighty *Anchors* from the *Bow*,
With *Ropes*, & *Ring-bolts* (where ŷ *Boat* was fast,
And we constrain'd to cut our *Mizen mast*,)
All lost at once : Afflictions now prevail,
And each mans heart and strength begins to fail ;
Sometimes we seem to *sink* sometimes to *float*,
The *Masters mate* tear's from his back his Coat
And stuffs between the *Timbers* ; then they cry
For *Bedding*, *Ruggs*, *and Blankets* eagerly,
Which when obtain'd they Crowd into each place
Where *streames* of *water* Issu'd in apace :
But all Industry seems without success,
The *Rageing storm* grows rather more than Less ;
Over those *Ruggs* they added *skins* of *Bears*,
And two new *Clothes* which our new *mainsail* spares;
Here may the hand of providence be Ey'd,
The *sayl* was made by those two *clothes* too wide,
Which by so much, we had made so much less
But a few dayes before our great Distress :
Ropes *Fore and Aft* were *streched* to secure
The *Mariners*, who scarcely could endure
Those *Big-swel'd Billows*, (what are feeble men ?)
So oft wash'd in, and out and in agen,
Sometimes upon, sometimes within the Ocean ;
The *Pumps* nev'r *sucking* tho in Constant motion ;
Whilst all the men and women then *on board*
With earnest Cryes did call upon the *LORD*
The *Seas* did frequently *o'erflow* the *ship*,
And we were often buri'd in the *Deep*:

The

The Chests *between Decks swim* as in a *flood*,
Where men up to their *knees* in water stood,
Expecting ev'ry Moment *grim look'd Death*
With that cold Element would stop their breath.

When suddenly a voice salutes our ears,
With Joy unspeakable amidst our Fears,
One of the PUMPS *does* SUCK! who can believe
What unexpected Comfort a *Repreive*
Brings a Condemned *Convict* : So that Voice
Caused each Cast down spirit to Rejoyce.

But on the *Fifth* of *February* we
Ship'd a prodigious *Mountain of a sea*,
Which with a pondrous and resistless Stroke
The Fixed *Table* and the Benches broke,
And with its Force Op'ned the *Cabbin* Door.
A weighty *Chest of Tooles* away it bore,
Then with loud Ecchos ev'ry Tongue declares
Our Period come, our Hopes were now Despaires.
For we lay *buri'd* in the *Oceans Womb*,
And might conclude it was our *wat'ry Tomb*;
But an Almighty power became our Freind,
Causing our *buri'd Vessel* to Ascend,
And by degrees climb up the *Mountain waves*,
From whence our *eyes* might view our *fluid Graves*;
Thus the Great God did Snatch us from below,
Unto whose pow'r we all our safeties owe.

Some few dayes after we a Ship might see,
Which *Coming up with* understood to be
For *England bound*, and from *Virginia* came,
Gregory Sugar was her *Captains* Name;

So

So *Leaky* (that tho they did what they could)
Sh' had *six* or *sev'n foot water in the Hould* ,
The Safety of their *Lives* they only fought ,
For to preferve their *Veffel* they could not ,
And *Hoyfting* out their *Boat* to come *a'board*
Which could not Safety to them all afford,
Yet *Thirteen* of them foon into it preft :
And *putting off*, promif'd to fetch the Reft :
When they came nigh our *Side* fuch fear was fhown,
None fought the good of *others* but his *own* ,
Each ftriving to preferve himfelf with haft ,
without regard to *make the Painter faft* ;
(Had they Endeavour'd , it had bin in vain)
The *Boat* fuch wrong and dammage did fuftain :
In *Laying us aboard* her *Bows* were *Stav'd* ,
That t'was meer *Mercy* any man was fav'd :
Soon the Difabled *Boat was gon a drift* ,
And now no hope of prefervat'on left
For thofe behind, who were in number five ,
For 'twas not poffible the Ship fhould *Live* ,
Nor with our Veffel did we dare come nigh ,
For ftill the troubled Sea *ran mountains high* ,
Tho their Intreaties, Peircing Cries and Grones ,
Might even draw Remorfnefs out of Stones ;
And now becaufe of the approaching night ,
We did advife them to *hang out a Light* ,
Which but till eight a Clock appear'd in Sight , }
After which time it did no more appear ,
And we concluded (as we well might fear)
They then went down : Tho we could not *relieve*
Their *wants*, their *lofs* we could not choofe but *grieve*.

And now some Comfort we begin to find,
The *winds* are *Calmer* and the *Seas* more kind,
Now Heav'ns alscourging hand its strokes withdrew
And former Consolations did Renew,
By giving us at length the *Sight* of *Land*,
By an Or'e ruling providential hand :
Our Cloudy cares appear to fly apace,
And Comforts seemingly supply their place;
The fourteenth day at *Plymouth* we Arrive,
With those thirteen we had preserv'd alive :
The nineteenth day for *London* we set *sayle*,
With not too much *wind*, but a mod'rate Gale.
But as if *Heav'n* with anger should reprove,
That we those mercies did not well Improve ;
Its *Breath* comes forth with *Fury* as before,
And we tho in the *Downes* and nigh the *Shore*,
Must feel more *strokes* of the chastising *Rod*
Of our offended of our angry GOD.

The Two and twentieth day much *wind* did blow,
When in the *Downs* we let our *Anchor* goe,
But it *came home* : we our Shift *Anchor Cast*,
Which (*insignificant*) came *home* as fast,
And we were driven up *alongst* the *Side*
Of a *Ship* there, which did at *Anchor ride*,
Our *Anchor* took her *Cable*, and did pass
Up with a speedy motion to her *Mass*,
Which at their *Bows* they *Cutting* from the *Cable*,
And t,other *Anchor* being too unable
To bring us up, broke in the *shank*. and we
Again (by Violence) *Drove out to Sea;*

We.

We thought to *Anchor* then in *Poulstone Bay*,
And let our *small Bower* go without delay,
Which like a rotten stick was quickly broke
(When once it came to strain) both *flewks & flock*,
Neither *Shift-Anchor*, *Best* nor yet *Small Bower*
To *Bring us up* had strength enough or power ;
And in the Afternoon the *winds* Restrain
Their furious *Blasts* , now only did remain
Our small *Cedge Anchor*, (unto which we must
Our *Lives*, our *Ship*, and all her *Cargo* trust,)
Which *Letting go*, Heav'ns care did so provide,
That we that *Ebb* secure in safety *Ride* ;
From which our apprehensions may Inspect,
How the *Great* God by *Small* meanes doth protect,
Whose strength can make our strongest *cables* weak,
Our *Cobwebs* strong, no earthly strein can break,
That we might put no Trust in *Earthen* Powers :
For weak is all the *Fortitude* of Our s.
An *Anchor* we that night from *Shore* obtain.
And so Return into the *Downs* again ,
And *weighing* thence , favour'd with *winds & floods*,
Our *selves* in Safety with our *ship* and *goods* ,
The *Twenty fifth* (assisted by the Lord)
Arriv'd at *London* and at *Ratcliff Moor'd* .

   Thou God of this great Vast, *that aloft Command*
               With thy Almighty Hand,
               Water , Earth, Air, and Fire
(*The Elements :*) *the* Sun, *the* Moon , *and* Stars
               Act not their own affaires ,
               But what thou dost require :
O who can view thy pow'r, *& not thy* pow'r *admire.*

Tis thou Alone art our alone support ,
  Thy Mercy's our strong fort ,
  Thou giv'st us length of dayes ,
To thee th' Almighty and Tri-une JEHOVE ,
  Dwelling in Heav'en above ;
  Be Everlasting Praise ;
O who can tast thy Good, & not Thanksgiving Raise.

A
POEM

OCCASIONALLY WRITTEN ON

Some Remarkables *hap'ning at the* Birth *of the* Son *of* Thomas *and* Sarah Wallis *upon the* Atlantick *or Western* Ocean, *July the* 26 1684.

WAllis, (for yet thou hast no other *Name*)
   This *Poem,* if thou live to read the same
In thy maturer years, thou mayst from thence
Ground Contemplations on God's *Providence.*
   At thy *Nativity* the *Southern Gales*
With Gentler *Breezes* faintly fill'd our Sailes,
The Curled *Ocean's* wrinkled Brows were down,
Whose Surface *Smil'd* that seem'd before to *frown,*
Neptunes Attendants from the *Deeps* resort,
And dance *Levaltos* in his *wat'ry Court*;
When thou wert Born, *July the Twenty fixt,*
Grampas and Sholes of *Porpoise* (Intermixt)
Attend the Ship, and *Pitterels* take Wing,
Both *Fish* and *Fowl* Advene the *Gossipping:*
And when the *Evening* of the day drew nigh,
The big swell'd Clouds darkned the *Azure* Sky
Shaking their dropping *Fleeces* on the *Maine,*
And to their Element return again ;
Lightnings bright *Flashes* issu'd from the Skye, ⎫
And *Peals* of Thunder Eccho'd from *on high* : ⎬
These things attended thy *Nativity.* ⎭

The *Climate* where thou thy firſt *breath* didſt draw,
Was between *Europe* and *America* :
About the *Latitude* of *Forty four*,
And *New-found Land* was judg,d the *nigheſt ſhore* :
The *Pinck Adventure* ſerv'd at once inſtead
Of thy *Birth-chamber*, *Cradle*, and thy *Bed*;
Hold not the meaneſs of the place in Scorn,
For *Chriſt* himſelf was in a *Stable* born :
When thy reflecting thoughts ſhall call to mind,
The Hardſhips incident to Humane kind,
Then let the *Eye* of *Faith* thy mind Convey
To view the *Manger* where thy *Saviour* lay .
Whom *God* hath ſent to bear thy *ſinfull load*,
Thou haſt no more to doe but *ſerve thy GOD* .
　　Now may the *Parents* of the *Child* enjoy,
Succeeding Comforts in their *Sea-born* Boy,
May his maturer years cauſe Joy and *mirth*,
Sweetning the *Troubles* that attend his *Birth*.
May they thoſe Conſolating Mercies prize,
As from the *God* of *Mercies* they Ariſe,
And from his *never-failing Fountains* flow,
To make their minds up to Thankſgiving grow ,
　　If the *Boy* lives and Capable to *Read*,
Tho the mean *Author* of theſe Lines be *Dead*,
Yet 'tis his will the *Youth* ſhould have the ſame,
And therefore, thereunto Subſcribes his name .

　　　　　　　RICHARD STEERE.

　　　　　FINIS.

The Daniel Catcher

(Printed by John Allen for Nicholas Boon)

Facsimile Reproduction

By permission of Mr. Frederick Lewis Gay, Brookline

Also in A A S.

The Daniel Catcher.

THE
LIFE
Of the Prophet
Daniel :

IN A
POEM.

To which is Added,
Earth's Felicities, Heaven's Allowances,
A Blank POEM.
With several other Poems.

By *R. S.*

Printed in the Year 1713.

THE
Life of the Prophet
DANIEL,
IN A
POEM.

How Rich, how great, how glorious is that Soul,
Whose *Faith* is stedfast, & without Controul;
Faith will the Temples with great Glory Crown;
Faith is the hand which takes the Blessing down;
Faith's the defensive, and Offensive Shield,
Saves the Possessor, makes th' Opposer yield.

  Antedeluvians, some in *Faith* Excel,
And thereby Liv'd; as Holy Records tell:

A   *Abel*

Abel, Enoch, and *Noah* in their Dayes,
By Efficacious Faith deserving praise,
Made th' Infant Earth Illustrious with its Rays.

Abra'm was call'd the Father of all those,
Who chuse that Life of *Faith* which *Abr'm* chose.
Isa'c and *Jacob,* Travell'd the same path,
And as his Sons by *nature,* were by *Faith,*
Moses, and *Samu'l* have the same pursu'd :
Who all as Stars of the first Magnitude,
Dart down their sev'ral bright Cælestial Rays,
Upon the Church in her more modern days ;
These all a Glorious Constellation prove,
Patterns of Faith, of Piety, and Love.

Can *Daniel* be forgot ? or may he come,
And with his Antecessors take a Room,
Of *Princes,* and of *Prophets,* not the least ;
His Soul with such Eximious *Faith* possest,
As stopt the mouths of *Lions,* Faith is Crown'd,
In that our *Dani'l* Innocent was found.

His History shall be our present Theme,
And from that fountain, we'll pursue the stream.
To paraphrase upon the state of things,
What Honours were confer'd on him by *Kings.*
His Life, Imprisonment, and Sufferings :

With what ftrong *Faith*, which did his Soul ad-
Working Miraculous Deliverance.   (advance,

Take then a tranfient view of him, behold
How his own Book, doth his own State unfold ;
See how the Spirit hath difplay'd the fence,
Of his Original, his Eminence.

He is defcended of Illuftrious Blood ;
His Pedigree was doubtlefs Great, and Good,
The Seed of *Princes* he appears to be,
Or fome prime *branch* of the *Nobility* ,
His Conduct, and his Courage, do proclaim
The greatnefs of his uncontrouled fame ;
For his great Soul, fo manag' all affairs,
As he did Antitype thofe Characters ;

Nor in the Series of his Lives whole Story,
Was *Daniel* found to be Derogatory,
But Ornamental to his Birth and Glory.
And as in Honour, fo in Beauty he
Arrives unto an Excellent degree ;
His graceful prefence perfonage and face,
Perfections vie with his Interior grace,
Each reprefenting him Lovely, and Rare,
So fairly good, or elfe fo goodly fair.

By Royal *Mandate* he's a Chofen One,
Attaining perfect Education,
In all the *Chald'an Learning*; he is taught
The Myfteries and Policies of State,
That he might ftand before the King, or be
A Privy Counfellor to's Majefty,
A polifh'd Pillar fix'd for the Support
Of Royalty, and Grandeur at the Court.

Yet he Religioufly avoids Excefs,
And frames his mind to be content with lefs.
The *Kings* delicious Dainties he denies,
With all the fulnefs of Court Luxuries;
For Pulfe and Water are his only fare,
Which to Great men is an Example Rare,

His humane parts, with grace divine wasCrown'd,
True wifdom and great knowledge did abound
In him; for he by God was Sanctify'd
To be a Prophet, whereby he unty'd
The Knotty. and moft Intricate of Dreams,
By pow'rful Influence of Celeftial beams,
Puzling Enigma's Vifions of the night,
He their Interpretation brings to Light.

He's

The Daniel Catcher.

He's Aptify'd for Publick Government,
Well qualify'd for Matters Eminent,
Faithful in Councel, and no *Sycophant*.
All thefe Concurring, fitted him to be
Intrufted, with Affairs of high degree,
Nothing Inferior to a Royalty.

The *King* Infpects his wifdom and great worth,
His favour then to honour calls him forth;
Makes him his *Lord-Lieutenant*, next the Throne,
Over the Province of Great *Babylon*.
More Honour yet, the *King* on him Confers,
Creates him greateft of his *Treafurers*;
And, as the *King* fhould fay, I cannot fee
One of more worth, in all my Monarchy,
Heaps Honour, upon Honour, adding more
Over the *Magi*, him Chief Governour.
To make his Royal Favour more compleat,
Daniel at Court is fixt Chief Favourite.

And now Involv'd in buis'nefs for the *King*,
(Honours and Offices do Troubles bring,
Yet) *Daniel* won't neglect three times a day
(As he did ufe) unto his God to Pray;
And while hisPrayers mount the Throne of Grace
All worldly Cares do to his thoughts give place

O happy Prince ! more happy in this Th
Whose Counsellors *fear God, Obey the King.*

Daniel Exalted now to High Renown,
Studies the only Int'rest of the *Crown,*
He knew his Lords great benefit would be,
T' have Officers of spotless Loyalty,
Men of an Equal Spirit with his own,
Were persons fittest to attend a *Throne.*

   This Policy of his appears to be
An act of unexampled Piety :
Next to his *Prince,* his Loyal Care Extends,
To shew some signal favour to h's Friends.
Great Comfort to the *Church,* in her Exile,
When *Nursing Fathers* on their *Children* smile ;
At his Request 'twas done, th' Effects were so,
For *Shadrach, Meshech* and *Abednego,*
O'er the Affairs of *Babylon* were sent,
To manage Grand Concerns of Government.

   See the Effects of his Industrious Care,
When such brave men in Publick Office are,
Whose publick Spirits, for the Publick Good,
Nebuchadnezzars Idols have withstood ;
Towhich his Princes, and his Lords of State
Pay Homage, whilst yet Inconsiderate.

Thefe men alone, with Faith and Courage kil'd,
Againft their *God*, and Confcience fcorn to yield.
They give a Check to th' Uncontroul'd Decree,
Shewing to *God*, and *King* Fidelity.
That Imp'ous Law, which like a Torrent flows,
(In honour to their *God*) they dare oppofe :
Tho' to the face of Inrag'd Majefty,
(Confiding in their *God*) they dare deny
The fulnefs of a Gen'rous Confidence,
In th' Great Pow'r of a *God* Immence,
Lifts their Refigning Souls fo much the high'r,
Before Idolatry, to Chufe the fire.
¶ So little difadvantage doth attend
On fuch, as on their *God* and *Truth* depend.
Such as ftand firm, to what they do profefs,
Wrap themfelves up in future Happinefs.
Such honour their *Profeffion*, and their *God*,
Whofe faith on *Kings* unjuft Commands have trod,
They in the face of Death, that King of Terrors,
By owning *God*, Convince the World of Errors.
With Conftancy, and Courage, fuch proclaim.
Triumphant Conquefts of Eternal Fame.
With what Affurance do fuch Souls Evince
There's none Infallible, no not the Prince ;

B　　　　　　　　　　　　　And

And he in Capitals may Read at large,
Such men will certainly their Truft difcharge.
And well conclude, in fuch he may Confide,
Who from their *God*, Refufe to turn afide.

What Service then did *Dan'el* to the Crown?
By lifting fuch to Places of Renown,
Whofe noble Tempers, and Heroick Souls
Their PrincesLaws,when againft *Gods*,Controuls
How happy is that Prince, whofe Grand Affairs
Are Lodged in fuch noble Breafts as theirs;
Who rather yield their Lives to Death, than be
Actors of Treafon, againft Sov'raignty.
Thefe are no pimping *Sycophants*, that win
Court Favour, by alluring *Kings* to Sin:
No, their brave Minds *Debauches* will Explode,
And all Leud Pleafures, that affront their *God.*
They'll rather have their Lives before him laid,
Than yield his Intereft fhould be betray'd;
E're they'll Difhonour *God*, or flatter men,
Or ftifle Confcience, they'll to *Fire*, or *Den.*

Thus Cloath'd with Grace, & Honours, *Dan'el*
Belov'd of all thofe, State Superlatives,   (Lives,
Th' Eternal Being alfo doth Refite,
Dan'el the Prophet's Heavens Favourite:

What greater Hononr can on Mortals be,
Than be beloved of the Deity ?
His Prince, that mighty Monarch alſo loves him,
For he a holy, prudent States-man proves him,
In whoſe high Favour he ſecurely Dwells,
Wiſdom, and Piety in him Excels.
In the whole Series of this Monarchs Reign, ⎫
What great Eſteem his worthineſs did gain, ⎬
Nebuchadnezzars Honour did maintain. ⎭

Alas ! what's this ? what ſweet Repoſe can be
Within the Arms of Earthly Majeſty :
When ſome at Princes Favours do arrive,
In their Eſteem, they no where elſe can Live ;
Thoſe warm Embraces of a Monarch's Love, ⎫
Chills their Devotion, that it cannot move, ⎬
To ſeek Repoſe Eternally Above. ⎭
Not walking in thoſe paths which *Dan'el* trod,
Who thought his greateſt good was nigh his *Gods*
For he conſults, an Earthly Prince muſt Dye,
Therefore ſeeks peace with *Divine Majeſty.*

And Piety can no aſſurance give,
He ſhall ſecure in Princes favours live ;
The leaſt Affront of Loyalty, deſtroys,
All hope of Comforr, in Terreſtrial Joys :

Or if by Death a Monarch be Remov'd,
The next Succeffor hates the man he Lov'd.
Dan'e! moft clearly doth this Truth Evince,
There's no fixation on an Earthly Prince;
When that great King *Nebuchadnezzar's* gone,
Dan'e! forbears Attendance on the Throne.

But for what caufe our *Prophet* did Retire,
Whether his *God* his Service did Require;
Or whether King *Belfhazzar,* difapprov'd
Whom his Grand-father had with Honour lov'd;
Or whether time had razed out the Fame
Of his Memorials, or obfcur'd his Name;
Or for what other caufe to me unknown,
He feems a perfect Stranger to the Throne,
Until an Hand without an Arm, affords
Strange Characters, both to the *King* and *Lords*;
For they Carouzing were in fluy'ous Bowls,
Till the Almighty's Hand their Mirth Controuls,
Which did with Terror fuch amazement bring,
To this fo Potent, but now Trembling *King,*
That ftraightway he for his *Magicians* fend,
Who inftantly on his Command attend;
But all in vain, for Mortals cannot fee,
Th' Interpretation of the Heav'ns Decree.

No other Spirit can the thing declare,
But his, whose hand did write the Character.

The Aged *Queen,* to the Young *King* doth tell,
Excelling Wisdom doth in *Dan'el* dwell;
Send Messengers for him, in him alone
Is found Divine Interpretation :
He's·come, *Belshazzar* greatly doth adore him,
Riches and Dignities are laid before him,
Which he, (as worthless) modestly refuses;
The *King* may give his Gifts to other uses.
Yet will he Serve his *God,* and *King* in this,
To let his *King* know, what *Gods* meaning is.
No Flattery from *Dan'els* lips will flow,
But the *King* shall his fatal Ruin know,
And who but *Dan'el* dares to tell him so.

The Clear, Divine, All-seeing Eye beheld,
That he the Scepter was unfit to weild,
When in the Heav'nly ballance he was weigh'd,
He was too light, the Scale turn'd Retrograde :
And tho' on Earth he was a Monarch Crown'd,
Fitter for *Tomb* than *Empire* he was found.
Esau his Birth-right greedily devours,
So this pronhanely drinks an *Emperours.*

No

No Cups ſo well could pleaſe his Imp'ous Mind,
As what for Sacred Uſes were Deſign'd:
Upbraiding Heaven, daring to defy
The Infinite All-Ruling Deity;
Having forgot the Generation paſt,
When's Grand-father with Beaſts had his Repaſt
Became a greater Broit, in brutiſh ſort,
Turning into a *Bachanale,* his Court.
Forgetting he was Mortal, and muſt Dye,
And paſs Account with Divine Majeſty;
No wonder that the *God Omnipotent,*
This ſudden Summons to *Belſhazzar* ſent;
No Variation in this firm Decree,
He who is all Immutability,
Signs with his Hand the *Kings* Mortality:
Yet e're he goes to his Eternal Port,
He will Exalt good *Dan'el* in his Court;
Thereby to bribe the Heav'ns, to Reprieve,
Or to Revoke the Doom that he might Live;
Dan'el, a Friend of God's; he did Eſteem
'Twas Policy to make *God* Friends with him;
Therefore Proclaims him, by his greatCommand
To be the third Chief Ruler in his Land.

But then alas ! What sudden Change,how soon
Low Earthly Glory, is from Mortals gone ?
Honours, and Riches, make them wings and fly,
As Streams diminish when the Fountain's dry :
The *King* that Night is Summon'd to the Duft,
Where his prophane Acts, do his Glories Ruft.

When next *Darius* mounts the lofty Throne ⎫
The *Mede* is now *King* of Great *Babylon* ; ⎬
Fame to his Ears, *Dan'els* great worth made ⎭
In whom was found fo Excellent a Soul, (known.
Whofe temp'rate mind,his paffions could controul.
The Aged *King*, by his grave wifdom, knows,
This weighty Crown will be too ponderous,
For his gray Head ; his Age confults his Eafe,
And therefore chufeth Sixfcore Deputies :
And over them he Conftituteth three,
The beft Efteemed in his Monarchy, ⎫
To whom all thofe accountable muft be ; ⎬
And of thofe three, although beloved all, ⎭
Dan'els Commiffion is for principal
The prime, and greateft Minifter of State,
And next Immediate to the Potentate.

His

His Honours now with greateſt luſtre, we
May in the *Zenith* of his Glories ſee ;
Now *Lord-High-Preſident* of great Renown,
Over the Councils that attend the Crown ;
And o'er the Treaſures of *Darius* State,
His Government, is next Immediate.
Nor did the *King* his favours thus beſtow,
But he had Reaſon for his doing ſo,
For his ſerene, and well poiz'd judgment, found
Faith, Prudence, Policy in him abound :
A Spirit of ſo Excellent a Frame,
That his Deſerts laid to his Honours Claim.

Dan'el no ſooner mounted is Above,
In full poſſeſſion of his Princes Love ;
No ſooner on the wing of Favour flies,
To Lofty Honours vaſt Tranſcendencies,
Tho' ne'er ſo juſtly merited, and Due ;
But Envious Rancor'd Sp'rits will purſue,
With eager minds, fill'd with Revengeful Hate,
What may Eclipſe the greatneſs of their State.
What between them and Honour (tho' Belov'd
By their great Sov raign) muſt be now Remov'd.

What !

What ! Shall an Alien lord it over me?
One of the *Children of Captivity*?
Shall we that are the Natives of the Land,
In our own Country bend to his Command?
Shall he Monopolize our Princes Love,
While we like Clouds below his glories move?
How can you bear, you *Princes, Lords* & *Peers*?
Shall *Babels* Honours be a Foreigners?
Let us Remove him : He once being gone,
Then our Access is nigher to the Throne.

　While many strive for Honour here, how few
Do the Eternal Crown of Life pursue?
Immortal Honour such a drug is grown,
They'll rather satisfie themselves with none ;
But the same Eye which for the one doth strive
Cannot the value of the other give.

　Methinks I see their Cabal Counsel, Croud
Under the Covert of a Sooty Cloud,
Shaking their *Plot-contriving Case of Brains,*
Taking all dextr'ous, and laborious Pains,
Gaping for breath, whilst others Lend an Ear
And each by Turns Commences Counseller,
This will not do, says one, th' other Replies
How shall we dress him for our Sacrifice?
　　　　　　C　　　　　　　Then

Then how they scratch their heads, and bite the
When this & that,& th' other counsel fails.(nails,
Are his State Ministrations all, so just ?
Can we not find him vary in his Trust ?
Let's his Attendants bribe, for they may see
Something defective in his Family ;
Can it be possible he Errs not, or ·
May not some words confound the Orator ?
May we not artificially Expound,
If but a doubtful Syllable be found
Drop from his Lip ? What ere th' occasion be,
Treason is meant against his Majesty.
Thus with malicious undermining Arts,
Their Consultation at his Honour darts ;
What shall we do? is there no hope to bring
Some guilty accusation to the King ?
Can we not find some colourable Story,
Diminutive t' his Dignity and Glory ?
Can we not dive into his inmost part ?
May not some Trait'rous tho't lodge in his heart
Which we might squeez into a Treas'nous sence,
And publickly produce for Evidence ;
But is his Soul too innocent and clear ;
And no hope left for an *Indictment* here ?
                                                Curs

Curfe on his Faith, his Loyalty, his truft;
Would he were not, unlefs he were unjuft.

Our circumfpection ought to be our care,
Which while unguarded, does invite a fnare;
For with our greateft diligence, we fcarce
Repel thofe darts that wou'd our honours pierce
Great Perfonages cannot be too wife,
For their Confpiring, plotting Enemies;
Whofe greedy Lufts, their Int'refts to advance,
Dare Swear men Traitors by their Countenance

But to their Honour, Let the world Admire,
They without Evidence could not Confpire;
Let it Remain unto Pofterity,
As a Remark of *Heathen Piety*,
Thefe Heathen Confpirators fcorn to foul,
With bafe Degen'rate Perjury, the Soul;
Tho˘ their Revenge fo fiercely they Engage,
Bafe Subornation muft not help their Rage,
They will not Damn their Souls, for thofe they
Foul Perjury meer Heathen boggle at.   (hate,

Rome doth from *Hell* fuch Imp'ous Cuftoms
As Confciencious Heathen fcorn to teach, (fetch,
Such monftrous births as thefe can never come,
But from that *Hydra* Tripple Crown of *Rome*,

Who Iſſues Diſpenſations, and Commiſſions,
Grants to the greateſt Villanies Permitions,
Rapine, Rebellion, Treaſon, Fire and *Blood,*
Is the Religion of that vip'rous Brood.
Can *Eighty Eight,* the Curſed *Powder Plot* ?
And *STROMBOLONIAN LONDON* be forgot?
So many Living Monuments appear,
Proves *Rome* more Imp'ous than the Heathen were ;
May Heav'ns dread Anger drive this Torrent
With all their Fry, to *Lucifer,* or *Rome.* (home,

    To their *Cabal* let us Return, and there
We find our Plotting Politicks deſpair
Of the Succeſs, in all they have deſign'd,
Nothing defective 'n him they can find ;
For his Allegiance to his Prince is ſuch,
They cannot *Dan'els* Reputation touch.
And this diſpair makes them conſult their wits ;
Since this, nor that, nor th' other project hits.
It is propos'd, and the propoſal finds
An univerſal one and all ; their minds
Concur, They at Religion will begin,
To find his Holy Duty to be Sin ;
His moſt Exact Obedience to his *God,*
Muſt be the Snare, the Trap, the Net. the Rod,

His dear Devotion, (which tho' he Esteem)
Must be the *Cord*, with which we'll *Strangle* him.
Get the Decree but Sign'd (the work is done)
Then let him Pray, and End what we begun,
Pray to the Grave ; each motion of his breath
In Prayer to his *God*, he prays to Death.
Will not this do my Lords ? shall we proceed ?
Nemine Contradicente : All Agreed.

  There needs no greater judgment upon those,
Whose Consultations do the Heav'ns oppose.
Who, against *God* their close devices bend,
His Honour is Engaged to defend,
Those who Conspire 'gainst Divine Majesty,
In their own Plots, shall their own Ruin see,
For he that shoots at Piety, and Grace,
Hits *God* himself directly in the face ;
That Malice which one single Soul doth wound,
Would, if it could, the Deity Confound.

  This new Contrivance hits so rarely well,
The honour of it doth so much Excel
All they have done, or thought upon before,
Th' Invention they are ready to adore.
O how they *Chuckle !* how they bless their wits,
 or being such Ingenious Counterfeits !

The Rare Intexture of this Plot, shuts out
All kind of Room for jealousie, or doubt;
It cannot miss, it is so strongly laid,
He must Deny his God, or be betray'd;
If he be just to him, his Life is ours,
This best Invention makes us Conquerours.
Thus the Decree, by general Assent,
Passes the *Peers,* as *Votes* in *Parliament,*
Who with unanimous Results agree,
And for Assent, Address his Majesty.

   They by a Law, Enact him God on Earth,
And whoso owns another, it is Death:
The *God* of Heav'n now must be deny'd,
And in his Room the *King* is Deify'd;
To him each Soul must his Devotions pay,
And to no other Deity must Pray;
For all Petitions must be spread before him:
They as a God for thirty days adore him,
Allowing *God,* as School boys for their plays,
An undivided month of Holy Dayes;
And whoso dares in thirty days to pray
To any other God, his Life shall pav.
O King *Darius,* thou art mounted high!
Who says you're Gods? When God says you must die.

Thofe Tributes due to *Cæfar*, I will pay,
But who makes man a God, doth man betray;
Thofe Honours and Prerogatives, which be
The proper Rights of Earthly Majefty,
I, in Obedience to my *God* will bring
And pay, as due unto my Sov'reign *King.*
But thofe, who *Kings* Exalt to that degree,
As they did *Herod*, by their Flattery,
Are none of *Cæfars* Friends, for *God* Above
Now for his Honour is oblig'd to move,
And with his flaming darts, and Arrows keen,
Make mortal *Kings* to know they are but men.

Darius ne'r confults from whence might fpring
The Branches of this new promoted thing:
Blinded with Honour and Ambition, He
Could not infpect his Nobles Flattery;
The Treacherous Defign was hid from him,
He did it perfect Loyalty Efteem,
Some policy of State, that might procure
A Grandeur to his *Empire*, more fecure;
That in his Glory he might brighter fhine,
And therefore doth more eafily incline;
Efpecially, fince he has but of late
Mounted the *Babylonian* Throne of State;

Thofe profer'd Honours he doth not withftand,
But the *Decree Signs* with his *Royal Hand.*
This Mortal Monarch, *King* of *Babylon,*
Juftles th' *Immortal Being* from his Throne ;
But his Ambitious, Daring, Rafh Defign
Calls from an Angry *God,* Revenge Divine.

A Rafh Refult, fuch may Repent too late
Who Anfwer firft, and after Meditate ;
To do, and then Confider is it good,
Or Anfwer e're the Queftion's underftood ;
Thus, I this fenfelefs fancy underftand,
It fhall be fo ; what was't you did Demand ;
Men may pretend great Politicks to be,
But fuch an Act is far from Policy ;
To do, and then to fay, what have I done ?
Would I had let this Stratagem alone,
Looks like the Fool defcrib'd by *Solomon.*

The *Plot is Laid, Sagacious Dan'el* fees
This an Intriegue laid by his Enemies :
His piercing judgment foon informs his mind,
That his Deftruction's by their Plot defign'd ;
In that Decree might *Dan'el* plainly Read,
His Execution firmly was Decre'd.

Yet

Yet 'tis below his Gen'rous Soul, to move
One step from *God* ; His firm Devotions prove
How little he doth dread their Stratagem ;
He bids Defiance both to it, and them ;
He scorns to live, Death he will rather chuse,
And will his Life, before his Duty lose.
E're he will want Communion with his *God*,
For thirty dayes, He'll pass that bloody Road
Which they provided for him, Their Decree,
Must be his way to Immortality :
If the true Ends of Life he cannot have,
'Tis not worth Living, *Better chuse the Grave.*
Death is the only way to set him free,
The Port that Lets in to Eternity ;
He will still Commune with his *God* by Pray r ;
Dan'el resolves to serve him here, or there.

No sooner had that Royal Hand and Pen
Sign'd the Insnaring Law, but these Great Men
Turn all Informers, greedy of their Prey,
How to Insnare, Trapan, Accuse, Betray
The *Lord High-President*, for he alone
Their Object is; he sits too nigh the Throne.

D   How

How do they *Sneak* about his Houfe, and *Creep*
Under the *Windows*, and through *Crannies* peep.
Methinks I fee how Covertly they ftand,
Each a Dark *Lantborn* in his trembling hand,
Their eafie footfteps, and their watchful Ears,
With their Dumb Signs, and Silent Characters,
That nothing might Impede, but that they may
Thro' their own filence, hear the Prophet Pray.
O how their hopes do fwell, their blood doth rife !
When they behold the *Cafement* open flies !
How their Hearts Leap for Joy, their Souls Revive !
In hope this opportunity will thrive !
And he, (Brave Spirit) fcorning to Retire,
Or to obfcure the thing which they defire,
Doth it on purpofe, to Confirm their Ears
That they, nor yet their Imp'ous Law he fears
But his Devotions to his *God* will pay,
And in defpite of their Decree will Pray.
The wings of Faith, and Zeal, mount him above
Fear of *Darius* Hate, or hope of Love.
Shall *Dan'el* his Beloved *God* Difown ?
Or wear a Mask on his Religion ?

                                        No.

No, 'tis below the greatneſs of his Soul,
To ſtain Religion with an act ſo foul ;
As not to do the thing he does profeſs,
He from his Principles will not digreſs ;
His Holy Reſolutions bear the ſway,
His *God* in ſpite of Mortals he'll obey-

No ſooner have their piercing Eyes Inſpection,
Of the leaſt motion towards *Genuflection* ;
When they behold thoſe ſacred joynts to bend,
How greedily tneir Eyes his motions tend,
How his preparatory ſighs they mind,
What they have ſought they now expect to find.
They diligently hearken, not for zeal,
Their itching Ears wait but for an appeal,
That they might hear his voice, ſo as to prove
It was directed, to a *God* above.
And tho the Heav'ns (as if the force they felt
At his Pathetical Expreſſions) melt,
A differentt Effect in them it ſeals,
Their putrid Hearts it hardens, or congeals.

Illuſtrious Prophet, little do we know
What various paſſions in thy mind may flow ;

Within

Within thy facred.breafts fuch thoughts may live
Nature 'gainft grace, grace may 'gainft nature
Or thou fo extafi'd, beyond the cares   (ftrive.
Of all terreftial, tranfient, low affairs.
Surely thy Soul flies upwards to its Reft,
Sweet Divine Raptures iffue from thy Breaft ;
Methinks I hear thy Heav'nly tho'ts Expreft.

   And muft I now forfake my *God ?* or pay
My Life to *Man,* if I my *God* obey :
Muft I, on fuch unhappy terms as thefe
Forfeit my Life ? or *God* of Life difpleafe,
Shall the confederating *Heathen,* fay
Die *Dan'el,* die, or Heaven difobey ?
Muft my Devotions hurl me to the Grave ?
Muft Prayer kill, which is a means to Save ?
'Tis worfe than death to live, one day alone,
Without *accefs* to the, *Celeftial Throne* ;
How then fhall I with thirty days difpence ?
What's life, when means of life is banifh'd hence?
Muft I upon my lips thefe Fetters wear ?
Muft my Affections, and my Tongue forbear
To call upon my *God* ? My Hope, my Truft.
No, let me die, e're I do prove unjuft.

Rather

Rather let Beasts a passage Tear, and free
My Captive Soul from its Captivity;
That it may to Eternal Mansions fly,
And take possession of Eternity;
Now let them rend me from *Darius* Love,
For that their Heaven is, but mine's above
My body is the *Kings,* at his command,
But my dear Soul is in my Makers hand;
To the fierce *Lions* I'le become a prey,
E're I my *Gods* commands will disobey.
The *Heathen* shall not Glory over me,
Nor yet Rejoyce in my Apostacy.
¶ Hold, Pause a little *Daniel,* do'st not fly
Upon thy winged zeal, a pitch too high?
Are all the sweets of Life of no Esteem?
Will not this *Daring Act* self-murder seem?
If thou destroy thy life, which thou may'st spare,
Will *God* incourage a self murderer?
Why wilt thou vainly, cast thy self away?
Is't not sufficient in thy thoughts to pray?
The Ceremony's but the outward shell,
Will not Ejaculation do as well?
God is a Spirit, if thy Spirit move,
He thy Devotion will as well approve;

What

What from thy Souls moſt ſecret Altar fly's,
Will be accepted as a Sacrifice ;
God the deſires of the humble meets,
And ſighs to him, from contrite Hearts, are ſweets ;
Mental Devotion to thy Soul is free,
Which countermines their Damn'd conſpiracie.

 Ah ! no, theſe weak temptations cannot find
Admittance, to appall his noble mind :
Daniel, to buy his Life, wont ſell his *God* :
But in thoſe paths which he before had trod,
He ſtill will move ; his Soul muſt ſtill have vent ,
His lips muſt call on the Omnipotent ;
He with his ſpeech his *God* ſtill Glorifies,
Tho his Deſtruction in his duty lies ;
Tho he ſhould Swiftly pray, himſelf to Air,
He will approach his *God* in vocal Pray'r ;
He'll rather to the *Lyons* be a prey,
Than but neglect his duty for a day.
And while his Enemies do ſtrictly watch,
He to his *God* in Prayer doth approach,
Regarding not his crafty *Obſervator,*
He thus Exalt, his voice to his, Creator.

         His

His Prayer Imagined

ALmighty, *and* Onipotent Jehove,
    Thou Glorious *and* Eternal God *above,*
Whose Habitation is Eternal light,
My God, *in thee* alone *is my delight* ;
O thou, whose fulness only does possess
Immencity, *and* Everlastingness.
Lord, what is man ? The son of man, that thou
Thy Glorious Ear to such an one dost bow ?
O how illustrious is thy grace, when we
Are made the objects of thy clemencie !
To thee O Lord, *To thee* Alone *I bend,*
O let let my Prayers *to* thy throne *ascend* ;
What is Darius, *Lord* ? *Whom men advance* ;
Can he, as God, *command Deliverance ?*
Such would invade the Glory of thy throne,
Who make their Deity a mortal one ;
A God they do adore, who cannot Save
Either himself, or others from the Grave.
Pardon, O pardon their Blasphemous deed ;
O let thy mercies, all their guilt exceed.
Though their design was principally Laid,
My Divine Priviledges to Invade ,

They

They would debar me from acceſs to thee,
They would Eclipſe that Glorious Libertie,
And draw a curtain 'twixt my God *and me.*

Lord, what is Life *to me, unleſs I may*
(Life *of my* Soul *) the* God *of life obey?*
Open the door of Grace, O Lord, *that I*
May to the Boſome of thy favour fly;
O let me Praiſe thee, let my only Aim
Be, in my Day, to Glorify thy name.
Lord, I am in thy hand, Grant me thy Power,
That over Death I may be Conquerour.
Give me a holy courage, that I may
Triumph in Death, e're Heaven Diſobey;
And let my Sacrifice Effectual prove,
To tell the world, Thou Lord, *who dwells above,*
Art the one, only God, *of Life and Love.*
Redeem thy Church ——————
—————— But then, O ſtrange ſurprize!
With vulgar tumults, and Exalted cries,
The houſe with loud Alarms is begirt round;
The horrid noiſe, his pure Devotions drown'd;
The Conſpirators, with a full mouth'd cry,
Bawl, Treaſon, Treaſon, 'gainſt his majeſty.

                                        And

And with a Guard, furprize this Proftrate Soul,
Whofe tho'ts were mounted far above the Pole.
Bring him away : *Darius* cannot Save
Him, from the Paunches of a living grave.
They without *Perjury* could fafely fwear,
He to the *God* of Heaven made his Pray'r ;
And now their Plot is to perfeftion brought, ⎞
They have obtain'd the only thing they fought, ⎬
For in the fnare the innocent is caught. ⎠

And now how Briskly do they pafs to Court?
Happy is he can give the firft report,
And to *Darius* Ears evidence bring,
Of one that Prays to *God,* and not the *King.*
But with what fubtilty do they proceed !
To make more fure what lately was decreed ;
They the Tranfgreffor do at firft obfcure,
To make the Law ftronger, or more fecure ;
They underftood the *King* fo well did love him,
Nothing could from his princely favour move him ;
He would defpence Prerogative, but he
Would fet his beft beloved *Dan'el* free,
If he forefaw, what they by craft obfcure,
His Royal Grant they once again procure ;

E.

The

That whosoev'r contemns what is Decreed,
The rav'ning beasts shall on his body feed,
This once obtain'd these Politicks proceed ;
One who pretends to Loyalty, and Trust,
Proves to your Sacred Majesty unjust.
Your Royal Law, which all ought to obey,
And as a Debt unto your Grandieur pay,
Is disesteem'd, slighted, and Countermanded,
As though *Dread Lord,* you had it not commanded,
One, whom to Honours you have lifted high,
Scorns to obey your Sacred Majesty.
Ungrateful Rebel ! Traitor to the Crown,
Which did Exalt him to so high renown;
His high disdain on your decree hath Trod,
And will not own *Darius* is a God,
But prays to something, which to us doth seem
To be at greater distances from him
For to the Heav'ns, and not unto your Throne,
He is Exalted in Devotion.
His vile, pernicious, Ill Example may
Intice your Subjects, in their minds astray
After some other *God* and so Deprive
Darius, of his great Prerogative

Shall

Shall he not Die ? Shall not the Law proceed ?
Hath not our god *Darius* fo decre'd ?

I cannot null, nor alter my decree,
Bring forth the Traitor inftantly to me,
And then produce your witnefs. Which is he ?

This *Dan'el* is the *Man* this *Captive. Slave,*
Who dares your Great and Royal Law outbrave.

Daniel ! Dear Daniel ! O, what have I done !
I Iffu'd out my rafh Refovles too foon ;
Ah ! you in this have rent from me a Jem,
Of Equal value with my Diadem.
My Soul is wounded, by this rafh Decree,
Which puts a' period to all Loyaltie ;
For in his breaft fuch Faithfulnefs did dwell
His unexampled Love did all Excell :
And muft I lofe him ? Muft he be remov'd ?
Shall I be difpoffeft of what I Lov'd ?
Ah! What diftraction wounds my troubled breaft ?
Of what I moft Efteem'd I'm Difpoffeft.
Who could Imagine that your fnare was laid
Againft your *King,* whofe Int'reft is betray'd ?

E 2

In this vile Act; by which is overthrown,
The strongeft Pillar, that fupports my Throne,
My Glorious State will Totter when he's gone.
This is fo far from Loyalty and Truft,
That it proclaims you hateful, and unjuft
To me, whom you in fcorn a God have made,
By which my only *Angel* is betray'd ;
What fhall I fay ? You're Enemies of peace,
Who hate what is your Sov'raigns happinefs ;
For I in him alone, was happy made,
But now, too late, I find we're both betray'd.
I was a *King*, would I have been Content,,
Without Invading the *Omnipotent.*
But I, too late, my Errours have Survey'd,
Darlas and his *Dan'el* are betray'd.

Unhappy *Dan'el*, thy unhappy State,
Makes thee an object both of Love, and Hate.
Thy King his Singular Refpects doth fhow,
The Nobles hate thee, to thy overthrow.
He, if he could, thy Honours would Support,
But they defign to tear thee from the Court,
For with a voice unanimous, they Cry
Deliver *Dan'el* to us, He muft Die

E 2   To

To Satisfy the Law ; why was it made ?
If *Kings* their own *Prerogatives* Invade.

The *King* Demurs, unwilling to proceed ;
His hand would cancel what he has decre'd ;
How willing would his Majefty Reprieve,
Although for once he ftrain'd Prerogatiye.

But fince their Plot hath had fo good fuccefs,
They will again Impat'ently Addrefs ;
Nor will they be deny'd of their Demand,
The *King* himfelf fhall not the *Law* withftand.
They (void of manners) Saucily proceed,
To tell the *King*, the Law he once decre'd,
He cannot Change, nay fhall not, nor is Able,
The *Mede* and *Perfians* Law's unalterable.
And though the *King* the *Kingdoms* Laws wou'd
We will be Satisfied to the full ;   (null ;
Dan'el muft Die : Why doth the *King* Contrive,
What by that Law is Dead, to keep alive ?
In vain *Darius*, thy Protecting hands
Strive to preferve, what thy own Law Commands
To Dire Deftruction, thou in Honour muft
Doom thy indeared Favourite to Duft

The

The *King Commands* ; but O, what inward care !
What grief ! what Soul fick trouble ! what defpair
Approach his Royal breaft ? He fighs,he grieves,
He Weeps and Sobs, when he the Sentence gives.
Ah ! Da- Da- *Daniel,* whom I Lo- Lo- Love,
Thy De- De- Death, muft Th- Th- Thee remove
The Se- Se-Sentence, I cannot deny,
Dear *Dan'el,* thou M- M- M- Muft Die.

And now Farewell, thou matchlefs Peer Adieu.
So bright a Star I never more fhall view,
Thou moft Illuftrious, True, and Loyal one ;
Thou greateft Treafure of an Earthly Throne.
Never was *King* fo happily poffeft,
Never was any Mortal Monarch Bleft
With fuch a Faithful Servant, fuch a Flow'r,
The only Glory of an Emperor.
But thou art mounting to Eternal Joys,
Beyond the Light, Low, mean, and Trivial toyes
Of Earthly Honours, where thou fhalt be bleft
In Glorious Manfions of Eternal reft.
Freely could I difrobe my felf of State,
And leave to be an Earthly Potentate,

To

To Change my felf to Spirit, and to fly
With my Dear *Dan'el* to Eternity.
But that I ftay behind to Sacrifice,
Whole Troops, of thy Invet'rate Enemies
To thy unfpotted, uncorrupted mind,
They my Avow'd Severe Revenge fhall find
Deftruction, as a Recompence I'll pay,
To thofe who did thy Innocence betray.
But ftay my thoughts. ————
———— Is not thy *God* the fame?
Who met his *Servants* in the *furious Flame*?
My thoughts perfwade me to a firm belief,
Thy *God* will fhew his pow'r, and fend Relief;
And, left thy Enemies the fame fhould fear, ⎫
And fo confult to fend fome Murderer, ⎬
More cruel than the Rav'nous Lyons are. ⎭
I, to prevent any fuch black defign,
With my one Signet, will the Prifon fign;
I'll Seal thee up, to the Protecting hand
Of thy own *God*, *The God of Sea and Land.*

How ftately to the *Den* doth *Dan'el* move,
Laden with Trophies of his Princes Love,

Cloath'd

Cloath'd with the Graces of his *God*, is he,
And Arm'd with Holy Armour *Cap-a-Pe.*
He nothing leaves behind him, that may seem
Needful, to take to Heav'n along with him.
Thoughts of Revenge, he doth so much defy,
That he can wish his greatest Enemy
An Equal share in Glory, with his own
Whose Malice sought his dire Destruction;
Those who did causlesly his Life betray,
For their Eternal Happiness he'll pray.

Now like an *Isa'c* is our *Dan'el* come,
Ready to pass from th' *Altar* to the Tomb;
Behold th' unspotted Sacrifice is drest,
On which the Priestly Lyons are to feast;
But to his wonder, and amazement, finds
Their Savage nature vary from their Kinds;
What Miracle is here ! This fatal *Den*
Presents more favour than inraged Men;
More friendship in the *Lyons Den* is shown,
Than in the *Royal Court* of *Babylon.*
A Glor'ous Spirit did his Soul invest,
True Right'ousness was fixed in his breast,

He

He was begirt with Truth and Innocence :
Thefe were his Arms, or Armour of Defence ;
His Adamantine Shield, he held fo faft,
As made him *Lyon Proof*; They'l rather Faft,
Nay Starve, than taft, or touch fuch Heav'nly *food*,
And Dye *with* thirft, Ere drink fuch Sacred *Blood.*
Civil, inftead of Savage, they Appear ;
They Couch, Submit, & fill'd with Awe & Fear
They Tremble, e'er attempt in Rage t'abufe,
Whom neither *God*, nor yet the *King* Accufe.

Thus *Dan'el*, in his Duty ftands before
His *God*, and *God* Demands of him no more ;
He yields his Life, his Faith to Teftify
And rather than be falfe to *God*, would Die ;
Whofe Life the hand of Providence protects,
He fhall not Dye, who thus his Life neglects ;
But he fhall freely keep, what freely He
Offer'd to give, it fhall Reftored be,
The Heav'nly Pow'rs ingag'd to fet him free.

The Royal *King*, in mourning Robes is dreft,
His thoughts abandon any kind of feaft ;

F   His

His Mourning Soul fasts for his best Belov'd.
Which Envy from him had to death Remov'd;
All kind of Mirth is banish'd from the Court,
No jovial Pastimes, no delightful Sport
Can have Admittance there; The *King's* in Tears,
Whose grief Creates Remorsness in the Peers;
No work for *Fidlers, Interludes,* or *Plays,*
Mourning is hung upon the *Poets* Bayes.
No *Singing, Dancing,* no delightful *Airs*
Are heard in Court, but doleful Sighs & Tears ;
The *Harp,* the *Organ, Flagillet,* and *Flute,*
The *Violin,* the *Dulcimer,* and *Lute,*
In Silence hang by, in the *Musick Room,*
As Rotten Ragged Scutcheons o'er a Tomb ;
The *King* now out of Tune, nothing can bear
That is delightful to the Eye or Ear ;
His thoughts Present him *Dan'els* Crys & groans,
Whilst Lyons Tear the flesh from off his Bones.
¶ But *Dan'els* Musick is to him more Sweet ;
While they lye Couchant, prostrate at his Feet ;
They so Melodiously, do *Snore* the Song
Of his Salvation, He can frame his tongue
To *Sing with them,* and lift his voice on high,
In *Hallelujahs* to the Deity ;

His

His joints, at Ev'ry *Snore* they breath, can move
And Dance *Corrante's* to the God of Love;

But all this while the *King* is Difcontent;
Alas! He cannot yet behold th' Event
Of this Dread Tragedy; he thinks at Leaft,
Dan'els Imboweld in thofe Savage Beafts,
Therefore his Princely Eyes can take no Reft;
Sleep is a perfect Stranger to thofe Eyes,
Before whofe glances Ghaftly *Dan'el* lyes;
And fince his beft Beloved Watchman's gone,
He cannot flumber, but will watch alone.
Ah! His dear *Dan'el* Sleeps in death, and fhall
He who did Love him, Sleep at's Funeral?

But all this while *Dan'el* Securely lyes,
Watching among his Sleeping Enemies,
And is become as a life Guard of theirs,
Who were defign'd his Executioners:
TheirGhaftly Eyes & yawningMouths are clos'd,
They-Sleep Secure, the Heav'ns *hath them* repos'd.
Mean time his pure Ejaculations fly;
His faithful Prayers mount above *the* Sky.

Behold

Behold a Miracle is here Expreſt,
The Sacrifice doth pray, and not the Prieſt,
He Prays tney may not make a Midnight feaſt.

No ſooner did *Aurora* bring the Day,
Driving the thick *Tenebrious* Clouds away ;
No ſooner were thoſe *Sable Curtains* drawn,
And dawning brightneſs mounts the *Horizon,*
But Great *Darius* Riſeth from his Bed,
To viſit *Dan'el,* if Alive, or Dead ;
The firſt approaching light his ſteps Convey,
A viſit to the *Lyons Den* to pay :
And, by his Haſty motion it Appears,
To Satisfie at once, his hopes, and fears ;
His Hope that *Dan'el* Lives, fills him with joys
His fear that he is Dead the ſame deſtroys.
Darius heart is in the *Lyons Den,*
And now he moves to meet his heart agen ;
How Briskly I behold his Royal feet,
With nimble motion Hurry through the Street,
His winged thoughts fly ſwifter than a Dove,
Yet can't Surpaſs the motion of his Love ;
He values not the Complements ot State,
Nor minds if his Retinue on him wait ;

                                    Nor

Nor for his *Coach or Chariot* will he ftay,
Left it fhould too much of his Time delay ;
If he can find his *Dan'el* but Alive,
'Tis Satisfaction in Superlative.
Might not *Darius* have a faith, which came
By its Original from *Abraham* ?
Who againft Hope, firmly in hope believes,
And ftrongeft faith the moft affurance gives.
What tho' the Lyons Beafts of Rapine are ?
And tho by hunger made the Eagerer ;
And what tho' Humane flefh & blood is Sweet ?
A noval Difh, and not their ufual meat :
'Tis poffible that Life from Death may Spring;
Sure, fome fuch faith as this poffefs'd the *King.*
He cryes Aloud, his voice the Air doth fill,
Dan'el ! Ho ! *Dan'el*, Art thou living ftill?

Hold, Hold *Darius*, ceafe thy hollow voice,
Leaft thou Awake the Lyons with the noife ;
Thy Loud Alarms, thy unexpected Cryes,   ⎫
May Roufe the Savage Beafts to Sacrifice,   ⎬
Thy deareft *Dan'el*, who among them Lyes.   ⎭
If they have fafted all the night from food,
May they not take their morning *draught* in blood ;
                                                    And

And break their fafts on that Delicious meat,
Which they laft night fet up, and could not Eat.

Brutes can no Reafon give for their Delay,
Their Savage nature is for prefent Prey ;
They cannot truft, but Run at all that Lyes
Within the profpect of their greedy Eyes,
Faith is a Stranger to their Rav'nous Claws,
Senfe only Cloys, or tires their Greedy Jaws ;
They think not of hereafter, or before,
But Gorge their Guts, till they can Eat no more.
The *King* well knew, if *Dan'el* mift their Jaws,
'Twas *Providence,* not *Project* was the Caufe.

The *King's* unchangeable Affections, prove
The greater Confirmation of his Love ;
His Princely favours pafs beyond the grave,
His faith, above his fenfe, what's Loft will Save
Through the Impenetrable Stones he Calls,
His Soul wrapt up in Sighs, doth pierce the walls,
And fafely doth arrive at *Dan'els* Ears,
Whofe joy Abounds, when he his Mafter hears.

Dan'el, what greater honour can be fhown ?
Was Ever Mortal Man fo waited on ?
                                        Was

Was Ever Pris'ner, when Condemn'd by fate,
Attended with such Majesty and State ?
Thy *God within,* Thy *King without* the *gate*
Waits in his Person, where he stays, till he
The Happy Prospect of his *Dan'el* See.

  Hear now this great and worthy Potentate,
Express his Soul, in Accents Paffionate.
O ! *Dan'el* Servant of that *Living God,*
Whose Habitation, Dwelling, and Abode
Is in Eternal, Everlasting Light ;
Whose Eyes can penetrate the Sable night
Is thy *God* able by his pow'r, to free
From Death. from Bondage and Captivitie
Such as depend on his Abilitie ?
Darius Queries, yet is far from doubt ;
His faith Confirms what he is come about,
For he Affirms, *Thy God will Set thee free* ;
His Confidence was in the Deitie.
Experience past Confirms his faith the more,
That *God* can do what he had done before ,
He the Effects of Faith doth now Embrace,
For Living *Dan'el* Stands before his face ;

Whom

Whom through the Grates, no fooner he Efpies,
The fudden vifion doth his Soul Surpize;
That in an Extafie of joy he ftands,
With Elevation of his Princely hands;
Being ftruck Dumb with Admiration, hears
His *Dan'els* voice Approach his *Royal Ears;*
In the fame Stile, with the fame Loyal Sound·
O King, For Ever Live. Live Ever Crown'd
With the Cæleftial Diadem of Glory,
When thou haft perfected thy Earthly Story.
Praifes Afcend from me, to God above,
That he the heart of my good *King* did move,
Thus to beftow on me his Princely Love
From Prayer he to Preaching doth proceed,
Tho' from his *Chappel* yet he is not fre'd.
The *King* Stands in the Porch, and doth not ftir,
But is Content to be his Auditor:
Into two Branches he his Theme doth bring
Leaving the Application to the *King*;
Firft he the goodnefs of his *God* declares,
Next his own *Innocency* he avers:
And thefe two Points doth he unite, to prove
The Mighty *God* doth Innocency Love,

　　　　　　　　　　　His

His Duty he from hence doth juſtifie,
Both to Divine, and Earthly Majeſty.
Such cannot be unfaithful to their *King*,
Who to their *God* are juſt in ev'ry thing;
Darius ne'er was ſatisfied more,
In any Sermon he had heard before.

The ſurly Lyons ſeem to underſtand,
And watch the motion of his Lip and hand,
How mute, and how demure they ſit and hear,
As if his voice were Muſick to their Ear ;
And if his Silence ſo much Aw'd their Sence,
How were they Charmed with his Eloquence.

Experience worketh Confidence, for he
Can the Beaſts Love, in his own Safety ſee,
Well may he truſt whom he hath found his
One Mercy on another ſtill Depends. (Friends,
The ſame Deliv'rance which firſt ſet him free,
Makes him ſtill Truſt in its Securitie ;
That which the *Lyon*, and the *Bear* Subdue,
Was the ſame *faith* which the *Philiſtine* ſlew,
The *Iſraelites* on the other *Shore* that ſtood,
Were *Sureties*, for all ſuch as paſs the *flood* :

G   So

So the same faith, as firmly doth Engage
Still to preserve, as first to stay the Rage
Of the fierce Lyons, till the Charm is past,
Which clearly quits the Innocent and Chast,
Who by his faith is justifi'd at Last
The *Sermon* being done, the *Seals* are Tore,
And open flies the *Stony Chappel Door* ;
The Captive Issues forth, where soon He Spies
His Royal Prince wrapt up in Extasies :
He's Heaven struck with Joy, and Admiration,
His Soul is wrap't in Divine Contemplation,
He like a Statue stands, fixt, and unmov'd.
His Royal Eyes gaze on his best Belov'd,
His Ravish'd Thoughts are glutted, with Excess
Of Heav'nly Raptures, which he can't Express.

After some Pause ————— Deliberately He
Doth Reassume the Thoughts of Majesty ;
And Thundring forth, with Terrour on his Brow,
Such Dreadful Mandates as must follow now ;
Orders for Executions forth are sent,
In Favour of his *Lord High President.*
Those who had his Destruction Late design'd,
Must the Revenge of great *Darius* find :
Those

Thofe who his Life had plotted to Betray,
Muft their own Lives, inftead of *Dan'els* pay

This Days Deliv'rance was of high Efteem,
When Heav'n beloved *Dan'el* did Redeem ;
And now the *King* refolves to keep a feaft,
In memory of his Reprieved Gueft ;
But the firft courfe he to the Lyons fends,
To make their fafting Appetites amends ;
They could not Taft that difh which firft was dreft,
Therefore the *King* fupplies 'em with a feaft ;
Variety of Sexes, Choice of meat,
Caufe on that Single difh they did not Eat ;
On which, when ferv'd, their Eager Stomachs fed
They had not patience till the *Cloth* was fpread
Dan'el gave thanks before : They flight the fafhion,
Falling on boldly without Invitation ;
They'r fo Impatient that they cannot ftay,
But meet each Courfe, while in the middle way
Before it comes to Table : They Devour,
And Drink *Carouzes* to the Emperour,
In the Hearts-blood of thofe Enormous Fiends,
Thofe vile Trapanners of the *Kings* beft friends

The Crackling of whofe bones their Mufick is,
They find no fweeter Melody than this ;
And having Supt, betake themfelves to Reft,
Well fatisfied with this Delicious feaft ;
Till they awake, and Roufe themfelves agen,
To overlook the Fragments in the Den ,
They Ready arc for more, if more there be
Found Acting Treafon 'gainft his Majeftie.
Thirfting with Greedy Appetites for Blood,
As thofe men did, who lately were their food.
Savage they were, and in that Savage State,
They juftly were Condemn'd to Savage fate.
It feems both Juft and Natural that thofe
Monfters in Nature, whofe Defigns oppofe
Their Lawful *King*, and Treach'roufly contrive
His beft of Subjects to Intomb Aliye,
That the fame way, they wickedly Invent
To Kill the juft, fhould be their Punifhment.
———————— Nec Lex eft juftior ulla
Quam Necis Artifices Arte perire fua.

No need of Procefs ; Summoning of Juries ;
He who Infalliably both juft, and Pure is,

Sits

Sits Judge.in Court, He who alone Surveys
Dark obfcure thoughts, untrodden Crooked ways
Of Sinful Mortals ; He who fits on High
Condemns, and who fhall dare to Juftify.
'Twas he thofe Caitiffs to Deftruction Hurl'd,
And by his Miracle Convinc'd the World.

It is a Maxim Politick in State,
And the prime Leffon of a Potentate,
To fix the Crown on his own Temples fure,
And in his Royal Throne to fit Secure ;
He therefore firft, Removes what may Impede
The Diadems fixation on his head ;
And if Confpiracy hereafter moves
So Lofty, as to Strike at what he Loves ;
Then Policy calls Majefty to Roufe,
And his beloved Subject's Caufe Efpoufe :
For fuch as venture at his Royal Breaft,
To Rend from thence, what he doth value beft ;
Will the next onfet, Ravenoufly fly
To ftrike the very Heart of Majefty ;
That Infolence which dares Attempt the one,
Dares undermine, or overthrow the Throne.

The

The *Great Darius* will Decree once more,
But not againft the Heavens as before ;
He'l be a *God* no longer, but Lay down
His Divine Title, for a Mortal one ;
His Divine Robes uneafie on him fate,
He is content with his Immediate State,
Tis 'nough to be an Earthly Potentate
For Heav'ns bright, fparkling glory, ftruck him
(blind
He could not fee what Treafons were defign'd,
Which the All-feeing Deity made known.;
Darius does himfelf as *God* Difown,
He will be only *King* of *Babylon,*
If he beloved *Dan'el* can poffefs,
Without Invading *Gods* Almightinefs,
Darius will Expeᵈ no more : But Proves
He *Dan'el,* and the *God* of *Dan'el* Loves ;
And Therefore fends his Royal Proclamations
Unto all People, Languages, and Nations.

                                    The

The Proclamation.

WE, Great *Darius King* of *Babylon,* (Throne
   Iſſue Commands, from this our Royal
To all the World, who on our Laws depend :
To whom the *God of Dan'el* we Commend ;
He is the *Living God,* that dwells Above,
The *God of Wonders,* the *Immence Jehove* ;
Who will protect, Deliver, and Redeem
All who believe, and hope, and truſt in him.
All *Liberty of Conſcience* we have given,
To worſhip *Dan'els God:* The *God of Heaven.*
The God of Peace, of *Unity,* and *Love*
The *Wonder-working God* who dwells Above,
Whoſe Kingdom, and whoſe Power, doth Extend
Infinite, Eternal, Glorious, without
                      End.

                                    Earth.

Earth Felicities,
Heavens Allowances.

A

𝕭lank 𝕻oem.

U Pon the Earth there are so many Treasures
Various Abounding objects of Delight,
That to Enumerate, would be a Task
Too ponderous for my Imperfect Skill,
Or Pen, to Charactise Effect'ally.
   Yet these felicities may be Reduc'd
Under three heads; As, *Riches, Honours, Pleasures:*
Whence as from fountains, All External good
Riseth, and flows to us in many Streams;
And whosoe'er posseffeth these, Enjoys
The fulness of all Temporary good.
   The good Effects which doth from *Riches* spring
Are not a few, nor of a mean Account;
As Education, Friends Acquaintance, Lovers.
With Dignity, Authority, Command,
And many other worthy our Esteem.
   From *Honour* comes Renown and Reputation,
Which when from worthy Actions it proceeds,

H   It's

It's still accompanied with inward Joy;
And brighter shines in men of Noble birth;
When they shall not Degenerate from those,
Their worthy Ancestors, whose virt'ous Acts
Lifted them to those Honours, and that trust,
Which gives these titles to the Name of great;
Nothing can more Imbellish noble Souls,
Than when their merits challenge honours crown.

Pleasures are many and of Divers Kinds,
Riches and *Honour* only serve to *please*;
And ev'ry good seems to this end ordain'd;
How many sweet felicities are found
Contributing to pleasure ev'ry scence
Visus, Auditus, Gustus, & Olfactus.

To please the *Eye* how many various Sights?
The fair and glorious Aspect of the *Heav'ns,*
The Darling brightness of the *Sun Moon Stars,*
The naked *Air,* the Curled Silver *Streams,*
The *Birds* Enamel'd with their Divers *Plumes*;
Orchards, whose *Trees,* with *blossoms, leaves & fruit*
Of various Kinds, all pleasing to the Eye,
The ev'n *Meadows,* in their Tap'stry green,
All Diapred with beauty blooming flow'rs;
The spacious *Ocean,* spreads her wat'ry vail
From shore, to shore, out of whose bowels come
Of sundry Creatures, Infinite in number,
As doth the Land afford, of Diff'rent *figures*:
Ships, Cities, Towns, Castles, and *Monuments*:
Gold, Pearls, and Rare Inestimable *Jems,*

                                        Do

Do all Contribute to delight the *Opticks.*

Likewise to please, & charm the Lift'ning *Ears,*
Sweet Muficks pleafant and harmonious Sounds;
The chirping notes of winged *Chorefters,*
And Purling Murmurs of the Gliding *brooks,*
Modulate Accents of a *well Tun'd voice,*
Joyn'd with the Sweet *Allurements* of the *Lute,*
The Gallant noife of Manly Mufick, *Bells*
Belonas voice of *Trumpets, Fifes* and *Drums,*
Pleafing difcourfes, *Hiftories* and *Novals,*
Am'rous Converfe, when Innocent and clean,
All give a Charming Sweetnefs to the Mufe.

Alfo to Gratifie the fence of *Tafting,*
Are various forts of *Flefh, Fifh, Fowl,* and *Fruits;*
Delicious Banquets, with their pleafing *Sauces,*
With Life refrefhing neat brisk Sparkling *Wines,*
Of Divers kinds, both Simple and Compound;
And many more unite to pleafe the *Tafte*

So, the *Olfactal* faculty's Supply'd,
With Oderiferous, and Choice *perfumes,*
Of *Myrrh,* of *Caffia,* and cf *Bruifed Spices;*
Sweet Smelling *Gums,* from the Arabian Coaft,
Or our Domeftick *Violets, Pinks,* and *Rofes;*
With Fragrant *Herbs,* & *Bloffoms* of our *Gardens.*
In fine, the pleafure of the Earth are fuch,
So good, fo many, Common, yet fo Sweet,
That fhould I Dwell for ever on Difcourfe,
It would furpafs the skill of Tongue or Pen,
Sufficiently their value to relate.

H 2

Yet

Yet let me add to these a pleasure more,
Of Loving *Parents*, Counter Loving *Children*;
. *Husband* and *Wife*, in Mut'al one-ness knit;
Friends during Life sharing each others Joys
Injoying Each the Others happy Love,
With Delectation : When we make our selves
Sensible, of the sweetness all affords ;
We may perceive a Possibility
By bounteous Heav'ns Allowance, on the Earth.
To find in Temp'ral good felicity.

  Having thus Transciently, in brief Survey'd,
Wherein all Earthly Happiness consists ;
To the intent we may therein be safe,
We with Content must fortify our minds,
That in all Stations, Accidents, Conditions,
We may Enjoy this worlds felicities,
Abstracted from the Ills that do accrue.
¶ He is the Richest, and most happy man,
Who is most moderate in his Desire :
Can be Content and sweetly satisfy'd
In ev'ry State, Condition, and degree ;
For he that Covets not possesseth all,
And may be truely call'd the Richest man ;
When he that has abundance, and yet fears
The loss or want of them, is truely poor ,
By his Ambitious and Intemp'rate mind,
Grieving for want of what his heart Desires,
Is in more Poverty, than he that wants,
Yet is Content to want, It grieves not him,
                                    Who

Who makes his little with Content Enough :
Whoso lets Loose th' unruly Appetite,
Desiring first a *Lordship* to possess
Then next a *Kingdom* ; After that a *World*
Which if he had, he would Account too Little
Or grieve, and pine, because it was no better,
Troubling his Restless mind still with desire ;
Such in no State can meet with Satisfaction :
Mind with how little nature is supply'd,
If we that little always have at hand,
We have as much in our Sufficiency,
As if possess'd with all the world affords.

    The silent Shade, the Quiet Country life,
Free from the Troubles of the *Crowded Town,*
Or the Perplexing Cares of State affairs,
And deep Projections of great *Politicians* ;
Under that bush where *Tityrus* did Sing,
Amidst the sweets of satisfy'd Delights,
With no more wealth than Riseth from Content,
This is a happy State : We often hear
The unperplexed plowmans Thoughtless note,
Tuneing his whistle to his working Teame,
In him behold the Emblem of Content,
A state of Happiness which we should seek,
Tho' Troubles cross the Road that leads thereto

    Crosses and *Troubles* Common are to men,
No one is free : *Crosses* sometimes he needs
To mix with pleasures, Pleasures else were bitter,
And wou'd grow Stale, and Cloy the Appetite,

But

But relish sweeter when with *Crosses* mixt ;
And tho our Troubles should be very Tart,
Yet being past we relish pleasures better.
    Wisdom and fortitude will us assist,
To raise our minds to such a noble Temper.
And fix such Peace, and Courage in our Souls,
That we shall dare to slight the *world* when't *frowns*,
And with Contempt shall look on its Insults ;
Scorning those Stroaks that Conquer feeble minds,
And thereby Crown our selves with Happiness.
    True Piety will Equally Contribute,
To make us face adversity with boldness,
Yielding to *God* Depend on him alone,
Who always what is best for us, will give ;
Subject our wills to his, Let the world frown,
We shall from all Afflictions be releas'd.
And relish Joy, when Sorrow's gone the better.
    Since there's a kind of happiness in Crosses,
Let no Condition find us discontent :
None can more Earths Felicities Enjoy,
Than doth the fearless free Contented man,
Who whether want, or have, or Loss, or gain,
He's of an even temper in all States,
All are alike to him, he's always happy
    Would we on Earth be happy, we must then
Use Earthly happiness without abuse ;
All our Intemperate desires will prove,
Disturbers of our Peace and happiness,
Griefs, Cares Distemp'red Passions, Anguish, Fears,
                                            Are

Are very Incident to vicious men;
They'r not Content with vice, tho it seem pleasant;
None like the virt'ous man can live Content,
He's most secure, lives Healthy, Happy, Free,
Pleasantly Chearful always Dwells in peace;
The Treasures, Riches, pleasures of his mind
Are Durable : In all things he delights,
His way to Heaven seems a pleasant path,
And all his Joruney as in Summer time.

   Let virtue guide us then in Earth Enjoyments,
Let *Temp'rance* teach us how to measure all,
Consult to use a mean, without abuse,
Both in the manner, measure, and the time,
While Justice leads us in the paths we tread,
Temp'rance (is like a Razour) Takes away
Those vicious Superfluities, that grow
Up to abuses, were they not Correct
By the Incision of its pruning virtues

   In all things we Enjoy, remember still
To send our thanks, to, whence the blessing came,
And let the Earths felicities Excite,
To move with Chearfulness in worthy Acts,
Raising our Thankful minds up to the fountain,
And with Divine and hearty Love Rejoyce,
That so by Looking up to heav'n above,
From whence these Lower joys to us descend,
We may a Heav'nly Paradice possess,
Of sweet and Comforting delights on Earth.

   That we in Earths Delights may find a joy,
Let's

Let's banish Superstition from our minds.
Could we Religions Excellency see,
We should be much Enamour'd with its Beauty,
Whose strict Injunctions no way does Impede
The Temp'rate Right and Consolating use
Of Heav'ns Allowance ; Earths Felicities.
   However Superstitious *Stoicks,* may
Refuse those blessings which are freely giv'n :
As if not making use of Earthly good,
Were to obtain Heav'ns Glory in Exchange,
And by a Solitary Ridged Fear,
Deprive themselves of Temp'ral Consolations,
Consulting all those Comforts to despise,
And seeming fearful of their sweets to taste,
As if within their good were Lodg'd infection :
And so deny themselves their harmless use ;
By which their fear, thro' weakness they have made
The world a grief & burthen to their minds.
Whereas without abuse we may, may ought,
Freely Enjoy Earths good in its good use.
Nature Invites, and Reason bids us tast ;
Temp'rance, as well Condemns Stupidity,
As Glut'ny and Excess it disallows,
Since both prohibit and deny us Comfort ;
We may Receive them, we are call'd to do 't,
They were Created only for our sakes ;
God freely gives them with a bount'ous hand,
To our necessities, while here we live ;
With mod'rate delectation, we may then

                                        Freely

Freely Enjoy, what God hath given Gratis :
Thofe who Reject a Joy fo good as this,
(Which Heav'n fo freely offers) are to blame.
  Such who Condemn the free & Chearful ufe
Of Earths Injoyments, do it for this caufe :
All Temporary Honours, Riches, Pleafures,
Are vain, uncertain, fhort, and Tranfitory,
And in comparifon of Heavenly joys,
They are not worthy of the leaft Efteem,
But rather to be fcornfully defpis'd.
  Tis True thofe Souls who often Contemplate.
The Heav'nly glories of Eternal Blifs,
Are above Earthly pleafures lifted up :
Such count Earths Joys comparatively none,
Or at the leaft not worthy their Efteem:
While their Bleft Souls afpire to heav'nly joys,
With fweet defires they do forget the Earth.
And Ravifhed with Superfweet Delights,
Seeming to feed upon Heav'ns Joys already .
And when their Souls are raifed to that pitch
They feem to Trample underfoot the World.
'Tis certain no comparifon can be,
'Twixt Heav'ns Eternity and Earthly time,
And in Comparifon of Heav'nly joys,
Earth's beft of Bleffings, fcarce deferve a name :
Yet in themfelves, and in Refpect to us,
And our neceffities, to difefteem 'em.
Would make us guilty of a heinous Crime.
They are in worth and time to be Regarded ,

As they're free gifts to us giv'n by the hand
Of God himself as Tokens sent from Heav'n
Not only for our needs, But to delight us,
Which may appear, because unto our sense,
They do afford us various Delectations,
Beyond necessity to Satiate.
Nor is this all, God doth not only give,
But lovingly Commands us to Enjoy,
Those Gracious Earnests of his future Love.
So that without abuses we may use them,
In their true use and moderate Enjoyance ;
Which may Attract, Encourage, and Invit e,
To all commendable and worthy Acts,
And raise our Souls to God from whence they came.
  'Tis certain there are many Dangers, hid
In Temporary, *Riches, Honours, Pleasures,*
Terrestrial Greatness, greatly may provoke
To all Ambition, and Intemp'rate Vice,
Yet guided by an Alsufficient Grace,
All those Impediments we may avoid,
And all into Felicity Convert.
When our Affections to those ills incline,
We ought with Reason, and with Grace consult
Such ill Desires to conquer and subdue.
It is more praise and glory to do well,
When in the middest of Greatest Temptations,
Than to be good for meer necessity ;
(Who in an Eunuch Chastity admires ?)
·And as the Dangers greater, so we shall
Greater Rewards gain by such Victory ;

Whereas to bind our selves by Sequeftration,
Thereby to fhun things Lawful and Expedient,
Which may, and ought with moderate Delight,
By us be us'd, becaufe there's danger there,
Argues a feeble and diftruftful mind.
    But for a man to know the higheft joys
This World affords, and yet without offence ;
To Live therein, and as a Mafter ufe them,
In all Refpects, and yet without abufe ;
One, who can as he lift Compel the World
To be his Servant, and will then do well,
When he's hedg'd round about with great Temp-
Certainly fuch a man in Heav'n, fhall be (tations,
Crown'd with the brighter Diadem of Glory :
What tho' no man can ferve two Mafters well,
The Supream God, and the Inferiour Mammon,
He's not concern'd, as being not the Man ;
This Man fubjects to one, Commands the other,
Owns God his Mafter, makes the World his Slave.
    'Tis further yet Objected, Abftinence
Suits beft, and fitteft to prepare the mind.
For Divine Exercifeand Contemplation ;
And next that many vicious Men Enjoy,
The Earth's Felicities, which Good men want,
Which fhews they are Impedements to Goodnefs
Alfo our Saviour doth exprefly fay,
'Tis hard for Rich men to Inherit glory,
And that the Meek, the Mournful, and Deject
Are rather Bleffed than Voluptuous men.

'Tis

　　Tis true, that Fasting best prepares the mind,
'Tis therefore requisite to Fast and Pray,
Retiring from the Pleasures of the World;
This is a Duty pleasing unto God,
And beneficial to the mind and body;
Purging our natures clean from sloth and dulness
Making us more Angelick, free and quick,
In the performance of our good Devotion;
It Aptifies our Souls, to Entertain
More Heav'nly and Divine Illumination.

　　But let Convenient Order be observ'd,
As there's a time to Mourn and be Deject,
A time from lawful Comforts to refrain;
So there's a time wherein we may Rejoyce,
May use and not refuse those Creature Gifts,
And Blessings, which our God so freely offers:
But in good order too, and times convenient
Using a Temp'rate Custom in their use,
That in their use we may attain their Blessing.

　　When by assistance of the Heav'nly Grace,
We can our minds unto that temper bring,
While in the fulness of all Earthly joys,
Which like our vassals wait on our Commands;
That how, and at our pleasure we may use,
And yet contemn them, when they intervene
Our heav'n born Souls, & our approach to Heav'n
Then notwithstanding all their Vanities,
Their Real Dangers, and Impedements,
We to their End may use them, and as such
May with content, with Chearfulness, & freedom,

Extract their sweetness with a Heavenly mind.
   Can we with *Lot* in *Sodom* live untainted ?
Or with our Saviour. Temp'rate mong sinners
When *Ouires* of *Syrens* Tempt to ill Designs,
Yet in the midst of all Allurements Chaste,
Is worth the name of Conquest, and Obtains
Vice-victors wreaths of Laurel : for whose brows
Crowns of Immortal honour are prepar'd,
Among those Heav'nly Inexhausted Treasures.
   Then Blessed are the Rich, the Great & Noble,
Whose Stations are above those Cob-web Laws,
Which keeps in Awe the Low and vulgar Crowd,
Yet can withstand the strongest of Temptations,
Provoking, and Enchanting, with Allurements ;
Such who have Pow'r to Sin without Controul ;
Yet in the Throng of all those Charming baits,
Can overcome Temptation in its pow'r,
Such Heroes Trampling on the Tempters head,
May sweetly Triumph as victorious Souls.
¶ That many good men want, what bad Enjoy.
May be to Quicken and Refine their Souls,
With Heav'nly Graces, and Increase their Glory:
In that Cælestial Happiness to Come.
That vicious men have what the Vertuous want,
May be to make their Misery the Greater,
With Greater punishment for Misimprovement :
Or ror what other causes, only known,
To the free Donor of all kinds of Good.
Yet many Regular, and Pious men,

A4

How great their Lord is, who above 'em dwells;
These but by Reason view'd, will make us own,
He is all VVisdom and Immence in Pow'r.
VVe with our Corp'ral Eye, can gaze unto
The *Spangled* Spheres,& *view those* Lights *of* Heav'n,
VVhose dazling, glorious, silver brightness, gives
A pleasant delectation; higher thence
Our Sprightly Souls, by winged Reason mounts,
To view the Impartial Throne, & Contemplate
Those Sence-Surpassing glories that attend it :
So that through Earthly Comforts, our dull Eyes
By Reasons Light, as through a Tellescope
May look to Heav'n, To God himself, and see
Some Glimpses of his Goodness, and his Pow'r,
And in some measure may already Taste,
Of those Reserved Sweets of Heav'nly Pleasures.
¶ But when we add Faiths Light, to Reasons Eye,
VVe far more plain, and clearly, can discern
God, in the mid'st of his Reserv'd Rewards,
Touching the Longing Palates of our Souls,
VVith fuller Cups of those Cælestial Joys,
And by a Spiritual conveyance feasts,
Our Ravish'd Souls with symptomes of his Love.
   How frequent may we find in Sacred VVrit,
Metaphors, Similies, Comparisons,
Drawn from these Temp'ral Things that are in
To signify to us Heav'ns unseen Glory, (sight,
As Riches, Honours, Pleasures, Kingdoms, Crowns,
Speaks to our sense the Highest State of Glory,
                                                    By

By such known Language Heav'n conveys to us,
High Apprehensions of Eternal Bliss;
Faith Exercis'd on these is of such force,
As to present our minds with future things,
Faith Soars aloft, and thence (preventing time)
Descends with Samples of those Joys to come.

    Let's often then by Faith and Reason Climb,
From Earthly Comforts up to Heav'nly Joys,
And Ruminate upon those Glorious Mansions,
Treasures, Crowns, Kingdoms, That Eternal Joy
Which we Expect hereafter to possess,
In him, in whom alone all fulness Dwells.

    The Poor, Despis'd, and Miserable man,
Hopes all his Comfort in the World to come,
Hopes to be Rich and Honourable there.
The Rich & Prosp'rous man with Reason thinks,
If he Enjoys Prosperity below,
And finds some Happiness consists therein,
He shall be much more happy, when posses'd
With Riches, whose duration never Ends.
Mount Contemplating Souls, a lofty pitch,
Upon the Soaring Wings of Faith and Reason,
To the Imperial Heav'n, To God on High,
Where of true pleasure thou may'st take thy fill.

    The Worlds vast Palace we may freely dwell in,
And let our Eyes, our Ears, and all our Senses,
Enjoy its Comforts with a chearful mind;
Since we have toleration from Above;
Still keeping pace with Time and Moderation.

K   Her

Her loweſt of Delights, are for that End
Created and Ordain'd; The Chirping Birds
Inſtructed in their warbling notes by nature,
Do Sing to pleaſe our Ears; whoſe Harmony
Affords to us a more Excelling uſe,
When we Contemplate on thoſe Heav'nly Joyes,
Which are prepar'd for us, where our Ears
Shall be more Bleſs'd with an Angelick Quire
Of Heav'nly Muſicks Lofty Rapid Aires,
Will Charm our Souls into an Extaſy.

   The Senceleſs Fountains alſo ſeem to ſtrive,
With their Soft purling Murmurs to Delight,
And Catch the Senſes with their pretty pleaſures;
Inviting us to think of thoſe pure Streams,
Whoſe ſweet Refreſhings glads our Heav'nly City,
And of that Springing, Inexhauſted fountain,
That whoſoever Taſts, ſhall never thirſt.

   When we Behold thoſe Glorious Lights above,
And ſhining Beauties of the Starry Orb,
Think of that Glory, ſo Surpaſſing this,
That could we Spy the Gl tt ring of one Ray,
 Twould Dazle *with* its brightneſs *our weak* opticks,
And we with *Peter* ſhould deſire to Dwell,
Where we ſuch Glorious Excellence behold.

   Or when we *Pallet* thoſe Delicious wines,
 And Curious Dainties of moſt pleaſing fruits,
Let them Excite our Appetites, to Taſte
Of thoſe Celeſtial feaſts, of Love and pleaſure,
Whoſe Endleſs ſweetneſs is beyond our thoughts
                      This

This Heav'nly Manna, This Angelick Bread,
This Divine Nectar, is so sweet, so pure ;
Did we but truly Taste thereof, we should
Be wholly Charm'd into a *Rapsody*,
Of Heav'nly Pleasures, Pleasures past Compare,
And in some small degree, our Souls might Relish
The sweetness of Eternal Joys on Earth.
 If thus the Earths Felicities we use,
Looking through them up to those joys beyond,
And so Enjoy them with a heav'nly mind,
We may in them feel heav'nly joys below,
That when our days shall Terminate, we may
From Heav'n on Earth, to Heav'n in Heav'n af-
Where our Felicities can know no (cend,
   End.

Antichrist Display'd

In a brief Character of the Sordid Ignorance,
and Implacable Cruelty of the Church of

R O M E.

Called in Scripture

Mistery Babylon the Great.

With the Certainty of her Total Fall, Final Destruction and Desolation, which produceth
matter for Sions *Ejaculation and Consolation.*

I Need no Heathen Deity Implore,
 To Charactrise this *Babylonish* whore ;

       She

She is Display'd Beyond the Art of men,
(As in Prophetick writings may be seen)
And might have spar'd the Labour of my Pen.
Yet as an Abstract of her Scarlet Sins,
My Muse her bloody Character begins;
Litt'ral *Babel* which in *Chaldea* stood,
Did Tipify this Curst Confused Brood;
That was, so this is in Confusion Hurl'd:
For Myst'ry Babel hath Amus'd the World;
As mounted on the seven headed Beast,
Her *Antichristian* Tricks make Manifest.
Frist view her *Legend,* so much doted on,
Each Cheat is counted Revelation;
Her Signs and lying Wonders, to deceive
Th' unthinking vulgar, making them believe
Her *Miracles,* Her false Delusions, when
They are indeed but *Jugling Cheats* of Men;
Her Sorceries and Witchcrafts, she Displays
Near the Beginning of the *Gospel* days
Encreasing more, and more, till the Black night
Of Ignorance, Eclips'd the Churches Light;
And by implicit faith, the People grope
After the Blind Dictations of the *Pope,*
And his Black Tribe of Locusts, which Devour
And Eat the Labour of the Labourer.
Thus *Rome* defil'd her Lawful Marriage Bed,
And by Successive *Pope's,* to Lewdness led,
Controuls the Dictates of the Churches head,

I mean the Supream Sov'raign, whofe Commands
She Difobeys, Contemns, and Countermands;
And like a Strumpet did Debauch her life,
Yet would be call'd the true and Lawful wife.
And when her whoredomes were Exceffive grown,
The Lawful Spoufe not only doth difown,
But with Revengful hate, and vaunting pride,
Arms to Root up the Children of the Bride.
Such as her vicious Actions did deteft,
Call'd *Proteftants*, becaufe they did *Proteft*
Againft her Curfed vile, Apoftate Sins;
On fuch her Fulminate Revenge begins;
And follow'd with a flood of Cruelties,
Her Averice to vaft Extreams did rife.
How did her hate, and high difdain break forth
Over all Chriftians She difplays her wrath:
Depofing Chriftian Kings as Hereticks.
Her Haughty foot treads the Imperial necks
Of Royal Monarchs, if they dare deny
Her univerfal *Popes* Supreamacy.
Moft fenfible all Chriftendom hath been,
That fhe Exalts her felf, to be a Queen
Sitting on many waters; She Difdains,
And as a Cruel Ridged Tyrant, Reigns,
Ov'r *Empires, Kingdoms, States*, All Nations are
Accounted Slaves and Vaffals unto her. (blood
What Havock hath fhe made? What Chriftian
Hath her vile Hands diftill'd into a flood?

In

In *Ireland*, In *Piedmont*, and *France*
She did her Scarlet bloody Flag advance.
And in the *Marian* days, by Regal Pow'r
What Crowds of Christians did her Lust devour,
In *Britain*, where in five years of her Reign,
Many a hundred Protestants were slain;
With studied Tortures barb'rous Acts were done
The like ne'er seen by the all viewing Sun.
Then fire and faggot was the Common Road,
For such as would not own a *Breaden God*;
Poor Christians suffer'd desp'rate Desolation,
By disallowing Transubstantiation,
Worshipping *Idols*, Altars; see th' events,
In famous *Fox's Acts* and *Monuments.*
Often her *Blood-hounds* did Conspire the death,
Of *Fame Renown'd*, Religious *El'zabeth*,
Our *Glorious Queen*, who forty four years stood ⎫
At *Englands* Helm, in spite of all that Brood, ⎬
Who *sought to* drink Hers, & *the* Kingdoms blood. ⎭
Look down to *James*, when he the Scepter swaid,
What plots against the three Estates were laid,
What Hellish Stratagems did she Invent,
Against the Kingdom. King, and *Parliament.*
Thence to the second *Chyrles*, cast an Eye down: ⎫
Tho She pretends great honour to the Crown, ⎬
Her chief design would have him overthrown. ⎭
Witness her hell hatch'd horrid Dreadful Plot
By Poys'ning, Dagger, or by pistol Shot.

That

That Prince muſt be Remov'd, it was his Doom,
And his beſt Subjects Sacrific'd to Rome ;
HerPlot was Rip'ned now to that degree,
Nothing Obſtructed her deſign but he ;
Could ſhe by any method take him down, }
That *Roman James might mount the* Royal Throne }
Their work was finiſh'd, & the Day their own· }
He falls ! He dies ! Alas ! unhappy Prince ;
A Fatal Appoplexy Took him hence :
Twas that diſeaſe ; (Tho Hereticks may doubt)
As ſure as *Capel* his own Jug'lers cut.
And now, what ſtrange Amazing Clouds appear,
Mant'ling with Sables *Britains* Hemiſphere ?
What diſmal fogs, and vapours, ſeem to come,
From ſome Cavernous Subteranian womb ;
Such crowds of Locuſts, from th' infernal ſhade }
Come crawling forth, in Roman Maſquerade, }
Britians's Priviledges to Invade. }
This was beheld by the All-ſeeing Eye,
Who in great mercy found a Remedy ;
Sends Royal *William* ; who, as with a Broom
Swept all into the pit, from whence they come.
Illuſtrious *William* ; with his Royal Queen,
Diſpell'd th' impending ſtorm, & drew the ſcæne,
Whom Heav'n Preſerve ──────────
────────── While we our Theme Renew,
And Antichriſtian Jezebel purſue.
'Tis this Inſatiate and Blood thirſty whore,
Whoſe Scarlet Robe is dy'd in Chriſtian Gore,

To

To whom the *Patbmos* Revelator, John,
Ascribes this Title, *Myst'ry Babylon.*
O view her Cruelty these Latter Times,
My Ink's not black Enough to paint her Crimes.
How hath her Rage 'whole Countries devasted:
Inflam'd great Cities, hath not *London* tasted
The sad Effects of her Prodigious Rage :
Both in the Antique and this modern Age,
This, this, and more a thousand times, we see
In those volum'nous Tracts of History :.
And all to Satisfy the Lusts of such,
Who wanting faith, yet Learning have too much;
I mean Her Crafty Priests, t' advance whose pride
Knowledge of God to others is deny'd ;
For they perceive, If People knew the Lord,
They to *their* Treasures wou'd less heaps afford;
But universally is *England* Blest,
The Sacred Truth is greatly manifest,
And Knowledge Issues like a mighty flood ;
As Divine Prophesies foretold it shou'd.
And shall this Drunken whore forever Reign ?
Drunk with the Blood of Martyrs, she hath slain?
Shall she the Kingdoms of the Earth Subdue ?
And Glory over those she Overthrew ?
Shall her Tyranick Monarchy Endure ?
Shall Romes Foundations always stand secure ?
No, no, Come out of her ye People all,
For God hath sa'd Great Babylon shall fall ;

Partake

Partake not of her Sins, leaft you fhould be
At laft confounded in her Mifery ;
Take Courage Sion, for the Pow'rs above
Have made a Refolution, to Remove
This Over-Ruling, Bold, Audacious Whore :
Down, She fhall down : And fhe fhall rife no more,
But as a Mill-ftone caft into the Main,
So fhall fhe fink, never to rife again.
Then fhall her crafty *Pybald Merchants,* fay
Alas ! Alas ! who thought to fee this day ?
No nation now our Merchandize will own,
Since our Great *Emporie* is Overthrown ;
Now no more fhrines are for *Diana* made,
We, like the Silverfmith have loft our Trade;
Alas ! Our fhelter mighty Babel's gone,
And in a defart we are left alone ;
What City's like to this ? whofe flames arife
Out of the ruine of our Merchandize ;
No more Prodigious vaft Eftates we gain,
It will no more fuch Golden fhowers rain,
Our *Tincy* will no more for filver pafs,
Now try'd by fire, 'tis Apparent Brafs :
Nothing will vend, (our coyn is all deny'd)
But what is fterling, and by Scripture try'd :
Such as will bear the Teft of holy writ,
And we Alas ! find ours is Counterfeit.
And though our Lord the Pope a promife made }
In Purgatory we fhould not be ftaid }
And fign'd our Pardons too, for which we paid. }

L   A }

All proves a lye : We liberty demand,
No.   The Crofs Devil cannot read his hand.
We therefore muft in thofe dark ManfionsDwell,
Which, but a thin brown paper parts from Hell.
The Pope has loft the Key of Heaven too,
And all our Roman art can't forge a new ;   (us
Who wou'd have tho't the Pope fhould *thus* deceive
To bring us to the Devil, and there leave us ;
Alas ! Alas ! where are our hopes become,
There is no Faith in man, no truth in Rome.

Ejaculation.

O Thou who fitteft on the Azure Throne !
   In thy own Time, caft down GreatBabylon
Thine and thy Sions great profeffed foe ;
O when fhall we behold her overthrow.
The fouls which underneath the Altar lye,
Their blood doth in thine Ears for vengeance cry
How long Lord God Almighty will it be,
E're thy ftrong Arm avenge her Crueltie ?
Return it Lord on her own head we pray,
Wilt thou fulfil the promife of the Day.
We, in fubmiffion to thy will, Intreat,
Knowing by faith thou art as juft as Great.
Blefs *England* ftill O Lord, that fhe may prize
Thy Providence ; and Antichrift Defpife,
The Pope and all thy Peoples Enemies.
O would the Sun difperfe thefe clouds away,
To ufher in the Glory of thy Day ?
And Gofpel beams *throughout* the world difplay.

Confolation.

REjoice O Sion, thy Redeemer will
    Each tittle of his Promifes fulfil ;
'Tis Confolation in a high degree,
When He, who's all Immutabilitie,
Declares his Refolution, to oppofe
His feeble Remnant's, ftrong and mighty foes.
He weareth Judgment as a Diadem,
And furely the oppreffor will Condemn ,
And take the Spoil out of his Rav'nous Pow'r
The Poor diftreffed he fhall not devour.
Chrift is a Comfort unto fuch as mourn,
Such as the world holds in Contempt, & Scorn ;
A father to the fatherlefs, is he,
And to the widow will a Husband be ;
He's faithful that hath promis'd, and will prove
Himfelf the object of his Peoples love ;
As he is willing, fo his pow'r is Great ;
No Stratagem can his refolves defeat.
Hence Confolation, to His Churches fprings,
When they confider, that the *King* of *Kings*
Proclaims this Refolution : He whofe pow'r
Surpaffeth all, whofe name's a mighty Tow'r.
Defpair not little flock : This will afford
Sufficient ftrength, and Comfort in the Lord ;
Build up each other in this faith, and then
Patiently wait till he fhall fay *Amen.*

Upon

Upon the Cælestial Embassy Perform'd by Angels, to the Shepherds on the Plains of Bethlehem, at the Birth of our Redeemer.

ANgels in Heav'n, as we may say,
 Keep one Eternal Holy-Day ;
No *Fasts* there are, nor *Vigils* there,
But Triumphs are their constant cheer ;
Yet when their King vouchsaf'd to come,
And make this lower world his home,
 They were so kind we know,
To come and keep one holy day below,
Sent on a solemn Embassy, to tell (dwell.
The world, how great a guest was coming there to

New Robes of Light, Heav'ns Liv'ry, they
Assume, more bright (by far) than day.
Yet not so bright as those, that there
The meanest Saint is us'd to wear ;
For they foresaw, it might undo .—
The lower world, to view them so :
  The Luster of so bright
And shining presence, would but scare & frigh
The Guilty world into Astonishment,
And fear they come to bring deserved punishment

But on a milder Errand these
Are sent, an Embassy of Peace,
Therefore they take a milder flame,
And with their beams unpointed came

Having Commission from above,
To Publish universal Love;
And being thus prepar'd,
That mortals at their sight might not be scar'd
Dreft in their Trav'ling cloaths; Direct the way
Unto *that diftant place where their great Sov'reign lay.*

Through rouling fpheres & floods of flame,
Swifter than fight or thought they came
Toward the laft, and loweft rounds,
Of the Etherial fpreading bounds,
Which parts the high, from lower world,
And from thofe battlements they hurld
Their Glances, to Survey
The lower Regions, and where *Bethle'm* lay
They fpy a little round black fpot, call'd Eartl
This they conclude the place of their great Sov'reigns birth

Cry they, Admiring then, is that!
(Pointing to Earth) that mighty Plat
Where are thofe fpacious Lands & Seas
Thofe mighty States, and Monarchies
That mortals brag of, where's that pride
Which has fo often Heav'n defy'd ?
And is the place fo fmall ?
What are the dwellers that about it Crawl ?
Our Prince made *one of* them; how great above
How *fmall art thou below* ! How *low the fteps of Love*

Down they decend, the clouds give way,
Thofe Regions all in darknefs lay,
Until their Prefence made it day ;

In fpite of th' interviewing fhade.
They by their beams difcov'ries made :
The Earth feems greater to their Eye,
As they draw nearer, Seas they fpy,
        What fpace the Oceans fill,
And *how the lofty* tow'ring mountains, fwell
Above the furface of thofe works of fame,
To *which the* lower worlds Inhabitants lay claim.

Cities, and Towns they fpy, & amongft them
Juries Metropolis *Jerufalem,*
In Fertile *Paleftine,* nigh which they view
Bethle'm a little Town : to which they flew,
This *is the place* they'r fent to, here they ceafe
Their *long fetch'd Journey, to make known the peace.*
       Which their great Sov'reign now,
Was come himfelf in Perfon to beftow ;
Such matchlefs condefcention as that,
Makes all the heav'nly hoft amaz'd *with* wonder at.

    Amaz'd, twixt fcorn and wonder, they
    Smile to fee how mean he lay ;
    That he, whom Heav'ns Immencitie
    Could not contain, fhould crowded be,
    And fhrink into the central point,
    Of the vaft univerfe, and ftint
        His greatnefs to a Place,
Of but a fpan amidft the Aiery fpace.
Will here, cry they, our Monarch keep his Court ?
Muft *this be now the place to which* we muft Refort ?
            'Then

Then to the Plains of *Bethl'em* they move,
There to Proclaim this univerſal love,
Not to the Prince at Court, but to the Swains,
Who *watch their* flocks by night *upon thoſe* Plains:
To them this Gracious Embaſſy is told,
Begining to Proclaim it thus BEHOLD;
(Amazing brightneſs drives away the dark
Hark ! Fellow Shepherds, Hark
The Proem is an Exce.　Exces are
Uſhers to things moſt Amirably Rare.)
GLAD NEWS, OF UNIVERSAL JOY WE
BRING;
THIS DAY IS BORN MANS ONLY SAVI-
OUR, CHRIST THE KING.

Gloria in Excelces

A Chriſtian Alphabet.

*Magnifying the Eternal God, in and through that
moſt Holy and Heavenly Man, the Lord Jeſus
Chriſt who is God over all Bleſſed for Ever Amen.*

ALL honour praiſe & thankfulneſs be given,
To thee, O King of Kings,& Lord of Lords;
Thou three in one, which record bears in Heav'n;
Who ſuch Tranſcendant love to *man* Affords.

BEhold what kind of love to *man* is ſhown !
To *man*, by Sin made viſer than a Beaſt,
Thine Arm for him hath wrought Salvation,
Tho of thy favours he deſerved leaſt.

C<a

CÆlestial love ! No Tongue Expreſs it can :
That *man* might live with God Eternally,
This love Superlative made *God* a *man,*
(O Love of loves !) & made that God-man dye

DID love for man do this ? And ſhall not he
Give up himſelf, in Body, Soul & Spirit ;
His Ranſome came from Gods own Treaſurie,
Mans all (the purchace) then let God Inherit.

EYE hath not ſeen *thoſe* Glorious things, O man,
Which God *in* Chriſt, *for thee hath freely wrought* ;
Would'ſt wear that famous Title *Chriſtian* :
Then be obedient to what he hath taught.

FEar God. This is the firſt & great Command :
Fear to offend him by commiting evil ,
Fear not but ſuch ſhall in his preſence ſtand,
Who by his light, and Grace, reſiſt the Devil.

GIve unto others as thou wouldſt be paid,
Do as thou wouldſt be done unto by all,
This Golden Rule unto thy Actions laid,
Serves well to meaſure neighbourhood withal.

HOnour and love, Fear and Obedience, are
To thy Creatour and Redeemer due ;
Thy neighbours welfare, next ſhould be thy care,
As ſaid that Tongue which never ſpake untrue.

IN thoſe (as ſaid that high and Holy man,)
Is comprehendad, (as the Total ſum)
The Law and Prophets : So the Ocean
Doth comprehend all Streams that to it come.

KEep in obedience unto thoſe Commands,
Whoſe reaſons give them a Perpet'al Date ;

Forbear to Act that which forbidden ſtands,
And live as one that ſeeks a future ſtate.

L ET all that can be ſaid, or thought, be done,
To ſhun all Evil, and Embrace all good ;
Yet we (unprofitable Ev'ry one)
Have, but as Servants done thoſe things we ſhou'd.

M Eriting no good for our ſelves to get,
No, all our good muſt come by Jeſus Chriſt;
Then let the reſt of our lives Alphabet,
Exalt his Glorious Merits in the High'ſt.

N O real nakedneſs was known to men, (then ;
Till ſin brought ſhame, then 'twas & not till
If man hath not Chriſts Right'ouſneſs, he will
(Tho clad in Silk and Gold) be naked ſtill.

O Lord ! Since mine own Right'ouſneſs, I find.
Too ſhort a Robe, to hide my ſin & ſhame,
Some of thine own (to cloath & change my mind)
Beſtow on me, then ſhall I praiſe thy name.

P Onder the man, new ſtarted from his ſins,
Juſt ſo much Light, & Grace Divine he hath,
(When he his Journey toward Heav'n begins,)
Dimly to ſhew him that there is a Path.

Q Uickly you'l find ſome progreſs *he hath made*,
Tho but a little now, a little then,
Having ſome ſlips, ſome falls, is much afraid,
Yet up he gets and forward goes agen.

R Is'n, as his light, ſo doth his courage grow,
He boldly now dares look *the* world i'th' face,

M And

And all its fears, and fnares, behind him throw,
As he finds new fupplies, of Light and Grace.

SIN in its native colours he difcries,
    And wars againft, Grace is the thing alone,
Affords fuch free and full difcoveries ;
He make it his Entire Companion.

TIll glorious ends, fhall all his graces crown,
    Making one conftant day, that *knows no night,*
O may tha graci us dawning not go down,
Till Grace, with Glory, fhall their Rayes unite.

UNto that Lord alone, afcribe the praife,
    Who put off all his Robes of Majefty,
And took mans nature, to give man his grace,
And to Reftore and fave mans life, did dye.

WIth the bleft Angels, man is now made ev'n,
    The fruit of love, tranfcending all compare
Chrift is fate down at Gods right hand in Heav'n,
And God and man in him united are.

XErxe-, who grieved that the Multitude,
    Should be Extinct in few years coming on,
Might have rejoyc'd, had he by faith him view'd,
Who is the Life and Refurrection.

YOU who are lovers of the Chriftian name,
    That Son of Righteoufnefs you will adore,
Our dear Lord Jefus Chrift, from whom it came,
Who once did rife from Death, to fet no more.

ZEal, faith, & love, fill your Seraphick tongues,
    Touch'd with a fpark from his diviner fire,
To chaunt aloud high praifes, Holy Songs
Whilft Angels Chorus in the Heav'nly quire.

On a Sea-Storm nigh the Coast.

ALL round the Horizon blackClouds appears
           A Storm is near :
Darkness Eclipseth the Sereener Sky,
           The Winds are high,
Making the Surface of the Ocean Show
Like mountains Lofty, and like Vallies Low.

The weighty Seas are rowled from the Deeps
           In mighty heaps,
And from the Rocks Foundations do arise
           To Kiss the Skies =
Wave after Wave in Hills each other Crowds,
As if the Deeps resolv'd to Storm the Clouds.

How did the Surging Billows Fome and Rore
           Against the Shore
Threatning to bring the Land under their power
           And it Devour :
Those Liquid Mountains on the Clifts were hurld
As to a Chaos they would shake the World.

The Earth did Interpose the Prince of Light
           Twas Sable nigh
All Darkness was but when the Lightnings fly
           And Light the Sky,
Night, Thunder, Lightning, Rain, & *raging* Wind,
To make a Storm had all their forces joyn'd.
                The

The Authors Option.

O Thou, who *Alpha*, and *Omega* as
 The spring, & root of all Created Things
One Ray from thee, to my Souls life impart;
Fit my Immortal Part with Holy Wings
To fly the World, to seek that Blest Aboad,
That I *may find that* Life, sure *hid with* Christ *in* God

FINIS.

Envoy

Envoy

THE foregoing sketches contain a few facts which have been brought out, and many suppositions which have been suggested, in the search for information regarding the author and printers of *A Monumental Memorial* and *The Daniel Catcher*; also, the result of an investigation concerning the Massachusetts press and printers in the seventeenth century.

The Club of Odd Volumes gratefully acknowledges its indebtedness to the Massachusetts Historical Society, and to Mr. Frederick L. Gay, for gracious permission to reproduce their precious specimens of the work of an early American poet apparently forgotten.

Richard Steere resided in Connecticut nearly twenty-five years, and while a citizen of New London wrote a volume of poetry which, although printed outside of the Connecticut Colony, antedates by forty-one years the *Poetical Meditations* of Roger Wolcott, which has the honor of being the first volume of verse printed in that colony.

Index

estate, 132 ; lawsuit with Glover heirs, 150-151 ; resigns as president of Harvard College, 151-152.

Dunton, John, his "Life and Errors," ii, 45, 62, 63, 64.

EAMES, Wilberforce, his "Bibliographic Notes on Eliot's Indian Bible," i, 228.

"Early Boston Booksellers," Littlefield's, ii, 69.

Eaton, Mary, i, 72.

Eaton, Rev. Nathaniel, i, 58, 63, 64, 103 ; chosen Professor in Harvard College, 62 ; his "Inquisitio in variantes Theologorum," etc., 65 ; his land becomes College property, 66 ; charged with cruelty, 67 ; flees from Massachusetts, 68 ; dismissed from College, 70 ; accepts pastorate of a Virginian church, 70 ; his "Oratio habita a N.E." etc., 70-71 ; his "De Fastis Anglicis," etc. 71 ; specimens of his verse, 71 ; imprisoned for debt, 72.

Eaton, Rev. Richard, i, 64, 65.

Eaton, Rev. Samuel, i, 65.

Eaton, Theophilus, i, 64, 65.

Edinburgh, University of, i, 251.

"Election Sermon," Rev. Samuel Torrey's, i, 265 ; ii, 19.

Eliot, John, Jr., i, 240.

Eliot, Rev. John, i, 73, 153, 211, 214, 218, 223, 224, 225, 226, 231, 232, 235, 236, 240, 241, 244, 246, 250, 251, 256, 265, 269 ; ii, 4, 5, 7, 8, 12, 77 ; his "New Englands First Fruits," i, 159-160, 167 ; his birth, 162 ; arrival in Boston, 162 ; learning the Indian language, 164-165 ; prepares a new version of the Psalms in metre, 165 ; his "Indian Grammar," 166 ; translates the Commandments, etc., into Indian language, 167 ; constructs a written Indian language, 167 ; preaches to the Indians, 168 ; endeavors to civilize them, 171 ; advocates schools, 172 ; his appeal to England for funds, 173-176 ; begins building Indian town, 180 ; preaches in Natick, 181 ; his "Indian Catechism," 191 ; his Indian Bible, 191 ; his death, 193 ; the credit of bringing the first master-printer to New

England is due to, 209 ; his letter to the Corporation in England regarding printing, 209-210 ; he recommends the re-engagement of Marmaduke Johnson, 226 ; mentions the Indian Grammar, 229 ; the control of the printing press committed to, 233 ; completes the Indian Grammar, 241 ; translates "The Primer," 247 ; the Indian A B C, ii, 4-6.

Eliot, Sir John, i, 157.

Eliot, Joseph, i, 240.

"Eliot, The Life of the Renowned," Rev. Cotton Mather's, i, 161.

"Eliot Tracts," the, i, 159.

Eliot's "Communion of Churches," i, 237, 238.

Ellesmere, Lord, i, 28.

Endicott, Gov. John, i, 39, 40, 58, 103, 184, 209, 210, 211 ; ii, 6.

"Entertaining Passages relating to Philip's War," etc., ii, 56.

"Ephemeris, The Boston. An Almanack for the Year MDCLXXXIV," Gillam's, ii, 25.

"Ephemeris of Coelestial Motions, An," Philomath's, ii, 18.

"Epistle to the Christian Indians, An," Cotton Mather's, ii, 55.

FELLOWS Orchard, Harvard College, i, 140.

Fisher, John, i, 111.

Fitch, Mary, i, 125.

Fitch, Zachary, i, 125.

Fleetwood, Col. George, i, 28.

Flint (Green), Mary, ii, 73.

Fleet, Thomas, ii, 66, 73.

Foord, Edward, i, 53.

Foster, Hopestill, ii, 3.

Foster, John, i, 269 ; ii, 17, 18, 19, 20, 28, 39, 40, 44, 54 ; graduates from Harvard College, ii, 3 ; interested in wood-engraving, 4 ; public writing master, 5 ; cuts the Colonial seal on wood, 6 ; prints "Narrative of the Troubles with the Indians," 6 ; engraves a view of Boston on metal, 7 ; buys Marmaduke Johnson's press, 7 ; prints "The Wicked Man's Portion," 10 ; loses the Corporation type and procures a new font, 12 ; prints "A

Brief History of the Wars with the Indians in New England," 12 ; his death and will, 12–13.

Fownell, John, i, 123, 151.

Franeker University, i, 65.

Freake, ——, i, 52.

"Freeman's Oath, The," i, 91.

Frost, Edmund, i, 139, 142.

GARDINER Family, The, i, 27.

Garrett, Harman, i, 110, 114.

Gay, Frederick L., i, 4, 5 ; ii, 81.

"Genealogical Dictionary," James Savage's, i, 197.

"Genealogical Gleanings in England," Waters', i, 21 footnote, 22, 37 footnote, 38, 42 footnote.

"Genealogies and Estates of Charlestown, The," Wyman's, ii, 39.

Genesis, Book of, printed in the Indian language, i, 186, 191, 200, 210, 218.

"George Bonaventure," the ship, i, 103.

Gibbon family, the, i, 41.

Gibbons, Capt. Edward, i, 35, 39, 40, 41, 58.

Gibbons, Jerusha, i, 40.

Gibson, Jno., i, 125.

Gillam, Benjamin, his, "The Boston Ephemeris" (1684), ii, 25.

Glen, James, prints Willard's "Covenant-Keeping," ii, 39.

"Glorious Progress of the Gospel, The," etc., i, 175.

Glover, Elizabeth (dau. of Jose Glover), i, 26, 75.

Glover, Elizabeth (Harris), i, 26, 28, 29, 35, 47, 49, 75, 85, 86, 87, 88, 89, 104 ; marries Rev. Henry Dunster, 105.

Glover, Jesse, Josse, see Glover, Rev. Jose.

Glover, John, his will, i, 22–23.

Glover, John (son of Rev. Jose), i, 27, 55, 82, 86, 142.

Glover, Rev. Jose, i, 75, 85, 86, 88, 91, 127, 128, 129, 130, 131, 132, 147, 150, 200, 205 ; ii, 8 ; The "Father of the Massachusetts Press," i, 19 ; solicits funds for college in Cambridge, 19 ; plans establishment of printing office in New England, 19 ; his marriage and family, 25 ; his second marriage, 26 ; connection with the Owfield and Thomson families, 37–38, 41 ; connection with the Gibbon and Pemberton families, 41 ; becomes a citizen of Boston, 43 ; purchases a printing press, 52 ; his will, 53–56 ; spelling of his Christian name, 66 ; his death, 56 ; Stephen Day gives bond to, 96–98 ; his management of the printing press, 102.

Glover, Priscilla, i, 26, 27, 54, 82.

Glover, Richard, i, 41.

Glover, Roger, i, 19, 41 ; his family, 20–23 ; his will, 24.

Glover, Roger (Jr.), i, 25, 26, 28, 55.

Glover, Sarah (Owfield), i, 25, 26, 27, 28.

Goffe, Edward, i, 63, 64, 78, 79, 80, 171.

Goffe, Samuell, i, 264.

Goodwin, John, i, 19.

Goodwin, Peter, i, 19.

Gookin, Major Daniel, i, 150, 234, 235 ; his "Historical Collections or the Indians of New England," 193.

Gorton, Samuel, i, 199.

"Grammar, Indian," Rev. John Eliot's, i, 166, 240, 241.

"Great House," the, Charlestown, i, 103.

Green, Bartholomew, Jr., i, 64, 65, 66, 69, 70, 197 ; opens a printing office in Boston, 206 ; ii, 29, 30, 36 ; in partnership with his father, 51 ; removes to Boston, 52 ; prints "Acts and Laws," 53 ; partnership with John Allen, 54 ; prints "The Massachusetts Psalter," 55 ; prints an "Indian Primer," 55 ; prints John Williams's "The Redeemed Captive," 55–56 ; prints "Entertaining Passages relating to Philip's War," 56 ; the printing office burned, 57 ; prints the Connecti- "Acts and Laws," 71.

Green, Bartholomew, Sr., i, 197, 198, 199.

Green, Elizabeth, i, 197.

Green (Butler), Hannah, ii, 26, 28, 30.

Green, Jonas (son of Timothy), ii, 69, 73 ; becomes printer to the Colony of Maryland, 74.

Green, Joseph, ii, 69.

Green (Kneeland), Mary, ii, 36.

Green, Samuel, i, 101, 128, 132, 133, 137, 152, 186, 191, 210, 212, 214, 217, 218, 221, 222, 223, 230, 235, 237, 239, 241, 250; ii, 39; in charge of the printing press, i, 192, 197; prints Shepard's "Sincere Convert," 193; his Cambridge property, 198; his military service, 199; his letter to John Winthrop, Jr., 200; prints "A Platform of Church Discipline," 201; the manager of the press, 202; prints the Laws, 202; his petition to the General Court for better equipment, 203–204; prints second edition of the Indian Bible, 204; takes his son into partnership, 204; retires from management of printing press, 204; the most famous of the early printers, 205; Marmaduke Johnson becomes enamoured of his daughter, 219; a list of books printed by, 246; his petition to the General Court regarding printing, 248–249; his name appears with Marmaduke Johnson's on imprints, 254–255; ii, 7; his letter to John Winthrop, Jr., asking aid to secure the Corporation type, 8–10; enters suit to get possession of Corporation type, 11–12; prints "The Cambridge Ephemeris," 25; assisted by James the Printer, 77.

Green, Samuel, Jr., ii, 39, 40, 45, 51, 64; prints for Samuel Sewall, ii, 18, 20; becomes manager of the Boston press, 21; prints "The Boston Ephemeris," 25; his petition for license to print, 26–28; moves to Milk St., 28; prints "The Present State of New England," 29; prints Mather's "Proclamation," 30; his death, 30; inventory of his estate, 32–35; a claim that the first newspaper printed in the English colonies was by, ii, 46.

Green, Samuel (son of Timothy), ii, 73.

Green, Dr. Samuel A., i, 133, 135, 262; ii, 4, 61; his "Ten Facsimile Reproductions relating to New England," i, 133 footnote; his "Ten Facsimile Reproductions relating to Old Boston and Neighborhood," ii, 13.

Green, Samuel and Bartholomew, print "Spiritual Milk," etc., i, 193; ii, 51;

print "Ornaments for the Daughters of Zion," i, 204.

Green, Timothy, ii, 61; the brother of Samuel Green, Jr., ii, 69; becomes the Connecticut Colonial printer, 72; prints the "Acts and Laws," 72; prints Bulkley's "Election Sermon," 73.

Green, Timothy, Jr., forms partnership with Samuel Kneeland, printer, ii, 73.

"Griffin," the ship, i, 198.

Griffith, George, i, 23.

Grout, John, i, 107, 108, 109.

Grover, ——, i, 225.

"Gutteridges Coffee House," ii, 47.

HAMPDEN, John, i, 157.

Hancock, Nathaniel, i, 91, 151.

Harris, Benjamin, i, 13, 251; ii, 46, 47, 52, 65.

Harris, Edward, i, 29.

Harris, Elizabeth, i, 26, 28, 29, 30.

Harris, John, i, 29, 55, 56.

Harris, Rev. Nathaniel, i, 28, 81.

Harris, Richard, i, 28, 29, 81.

Harris, Vavasour, ii, 53, 54, 65.

Harvard Hall, i, 81, 103.

Harvard, Rev. John, i, 58; his legacy to Harvard College, 62, 63, 72, 103.

Harvard University, i, 30, 33; Rev. Jose Glover solicits funds for establishing college, 19; Gov. Edward Hopkins bequeaths money to, 37; the selection of executive officer considered, 50–51; site selected, 61; given its name, 61; early records in "College Books," 62; Nathaniel Eaton chosen Professor, 62; Cambridge grants land, 65–66; Nathaniel Eaton dismissed, 70; Rev. Henry Dunster assumes the presidency, 72; house for President ordered built, 75; Richard Harris appointed instructor, 81–82; the printing office part of the college, 85; Dunster MSS. 96; Fellows Orchard, 140; Matthew Day the steward of, 140; Matthew Day gives land to, 141; relation of the printing press to, 147; press removed to, 149; incorporation of, 150; Rev. Henry Dunster resigns as president of, 151–152; Rev. Charles Chauncy, president, 152; training of Indians, and erecting of special

RETURN **LIBRARY SCHOOL LIBRARY**
TO ➡ 2 South Hall   642-2253

LOAN PERIOD 1	2	3
4	5	6

ALL BOOKS MAY BE RECALLED AFTER 7 DAYS

DUE AS STAMPED BELOW

MAR 2 3 1979		
MAR 1 8 1983		
JUN 1 1 1983		

FORM NO. DD 18, 45m, 6'76   UNIVERSITY OF CALIFORNIA, BERKELEY
BERKELEY, CA 94720